Lecture Notes in Computer Science 3031

Commenced Publication in 1973
Founding and Former Series Editors:
Gerhard Goos, Juris Hartmanis, and Jan van Leeuwen

Editorial Board:

Takeo Kanade
  Carnegie Mellon University, Pittsburgh, PA, USA
Josef Kittler
  University of Surrey, Guildford, UK
Jon M. Kleinberg
  Cornell University, Ithaca, NY, USA
Friedemann Mattern
  ETH Zurich, Switzerland
John C. Mitchell
  Stanford University, CA, USA
Oscar Nierstrasz
  University of Berne, Switzerland
C. Pandu Rangan
  Indian Institute of Technology, Madras, India
Bernhard Steffen
  Dortmund University, Germany
Demetri Terzopoulos
  New York University, NY, USA
Doug Tygar
  University of California at Berkeley, CA, USA
Moshe Y. Vardi
  Rice University, Houston, TX, USA

Springer
Berlin
Heidelberg
New York
Hong Kong
London
Milan
Paris
Tokyo

Andreas Butz   Antonio Krüger
Patrick Olivier (Eds.)

Smart Graphics

4th International Symposium, SG 2004
Banff, Canada, May 23-25, 2004
Proceedings

Springer

Volume Editors

Andreas Butz
Antonio Krüger
Department of Computer Science, Saarland University
Stuhlsatzenhausweg, Bau 36.1
66123 Saarbrücken, Germany
E-mail: {butz,krueger}@cs.uni-sb.de

Patrick Olivier
Lexicle Ltd.
Innovation Center, York Science Park, York, YO10 5DG, UK
E-mail: plo@lexicle.com

Library of Congress Control Number: 2004105605

CR Subject Classification (1998): I.3, I.2.10, I.2, I.4, I.5, H.5, I.7

ISSN 0302-9743
ISBN 3-540-21977-3 Springer-Verlag Berlin Heidelberg New York

This work is subject to copyright. All rights are reserved, whether the whole or part of the material is concerned, specifically the rights of translation, reprinting, re-use of illustrations, recitation, broadcasting, reproduction on microfilms or in any other way, and storage in data banks. Duplication of this publication or parts thereof is permitted only under the provisions of the German Copyright Law of September 9, 1965, in its current version, and permission for use must always be obtained from Springer-Verlag. Violations are liable to prosecution under the German Copyright Law.

Springer-Verlag is a part of Springer Science+Business Media

springeronline.com

© Springer-Verlag Berlin Heidelberg 2004
Printed in Germany

Typesetting: Camera-ready by author, data conversion by Boller Mediendesign
Printed on acid-free paper   SPIN: 11005919   06/3142   5 4 3 2 1 0

Preface

The International Symposium on Smart Graphics 2004 was held on May 23–25, 2004 in Banff, Canada. It was the fifth event in a series which originally started in 2000 as a AAAI Spring Symposium. In response to the overwhelming success of the 2000 symposium, its organizers decided to turn it into a self-contained event in 2001. With the support of IBM, the first two International Symposia on Smart Graphics were held at the T.J. Watson Research Center in Hawthorne, NY in 2001 and 2002. The 2003 symposium moved to the European Media Lab in Heidelberg to underline the international character of the Smart Graphics enterprise and its community. The 2004 symposium particularly emphasized the contribution of arts and design to the interdisciplinary field of Smart Graphics and was therefore held at the Banff Centre in Alberta, Canada, an internationally recognized center of creative excellence.

The core idea behind these symposia is to bring together researchers and practitioners from the field of computer graphics, artificial intelligence, cognitive psychology and the fine arts. Each of these disciplines contributes to what we mean by the term "Smart Graphics": the intelligent process of creating expressive and esthetic graphical presentations. While artists and designers have been creating communicative graphics for centuries, artificial intelligence focuses on automating this process by means of the computer. While computer graphics provides the tools for creating graphical presentations in the first place, cognitive sciences contribute the rules and models of perception necessary for the design of effective graphics. The exchange of ideas between these four disciplines has led to many exciting and fruitful discussions and the Smart Graphics symposia draw their liveliness from a spirit of open minds and the willingness to learn from and share with other disciplines.

We would like to thank all authors for the effort that went into their submissions, the program committee for their work in selecting and ordering contributions for the final program, the Banff Centre and our local organizers for providing space and time for hosting the event, and Springer-Verlag Heidelberg for publishing the proceedings in their Lecture Notes in Computer Science.

March 2004

Andreas Butz
Antonio Krüger
Patrick Olivier

Organization

Organizing Committee

Conference Chairs   Andreas Butz (Saarland University, Germany)
                                Antonio Krüger (Saarland University, Germany)
                                Patrick Olivier (Lexicle Limited, UK)
Local Organization   Sara Diamond (Banff Centre, Canada)
                                Brian Fisher (University of British Columbia, Canada)

Program Committee

Maneesh Agrawala (Microsoft Research, USA)
Elisabeth André (University of Augsburg, Germany)
Steven Feiner (Columbia University, New York, USA)
Sidney Fels (University of British Columbia, Canada)
Mark Hansen (University of California, Los Angeles, USA)
Knut Hartmann (University of Magdeburg, Germany)
Takeo Igarashi (University of Tokyo, Japan)
Rainer Malaka (European Media Lab, Germany)
W. Bradford Paley (Digital Image Design, USA)
Bernhard Preim (University of Magdeburg, Germany)
Thomas Rist (DFKI Saarbrücken, Germany)
Andrew Salway (University of Surrey, UK)
Stefan Schlechtweg (University of Magdeburg, Germany)
Sha Xinwei (Georgia Institute of Technology, USA)
Massimo Zancanaro (ITC-IRST Trento, Italy)
Michelle Zhou (IBM T.J. Watson Research Center, USA)

Secondary Reviewers

Blaine Bell, Columbia University
Hrvoje Benko, Columbia University
James T. Klosowski, IBM

Sponsoring Institutions

The 4th International Symposium on Smart Graphics was hosted at the Banff Centre in Alberta, Canada. Organizational support was given by the Banff New Media Institute (BNMI).

Table of Contents

Virtual Characters and Environments

Tangible and Hybrid Interfaces

Graphical Interfaces

Poster Presentations

Animating 2D Digital Puppets with Limited Autonomy

Erin Shaw, Catherine LaBore, Yuan-Chun Chiu, and W. Lewis Johnson

Center for Advanced Research in Technology for Education
4676 Admiralty Way, Marina del Rey, 90292, USA
{shaw, labore, joechiu, johnson}@isi.edu
http://www.isi.edu/isd/carte/index.html

Abstract. Digital puppets are animated personas that augment online educational materials with commentary and summaries. Their animations are generated dynamically based on user-authored text, contextual hints, and domain goals, allowing the puppet to act with limited autonomy within specific domains. In this paper we describe the graphical realization and authoring of a 2D digital puppet. We present a *build-once, use-forever* production path that allows us to quickly create new character behaviors, and makes the production of 2D personas feasible. We describe two digital puppet applications and explain how the animation capability is supported across domains.

1 Introduction

Animated characters are becoming increasingly popular for use in conversational interfaces, and as presentation and pedagogical agents. In this paper we describe the graphical realization and authoring of a animated character, or Digital Puppet, which can act with limited autonomy in its particular domain. Digital Puppets augment online educational materials with commentary and summaries, and have been used in both the tutoring and the presentation domain. The work presented here is builds upon our experiences creating pedagogical animated characters, or *guidebots* [19][20][24][28][12][15]. Like guidebots, digital puppets interact with learners via a combination of speech and gestures, making it possible to more accurately model the kinds of dialogs and interactions that occur during apprenticeship learning and one-on-one tutoring. They personify the interface, building upon people's natural tendency to interact socially with computers [23], and can express both thoughts and emotions, in order to portray enthusiasm and empathy. Like real expert tutors that attend to both motivational and cognitive factors, animated characters have the potential to increase learner curiosity and interest, and to offer help and reassurance when they encounter difficulties [16].

The digital puppet system, and in particular, its animation and authoring, is motivated by two drawbacks to developing agents in a research environment: limited budgets and the prototype development cycle. First, we have found limited-animation 2D characters particularly useful for some pedagogical applications; cartoon 2D for younger children and realistic 2D for adult storytelling. However,

A. Butz et al. (Eds.): SG 2004, LNCS 3031, pp. 1–10, 2004.
© Springer-Verlag Berlin Heidelberg 2004

production demands for animated characters frequently exceed limited research budgets. This is especially true for complex characters, like the puppets, that are designed to speak and gesture in parallel. To make the production of 2D personas feasible, we have developed a *build-once, use-forever* production path that allows us to quickly create new behaviors for a given character [set]. Second, we have found that the prototype iteration cycle for agents precludes a broad focus: Only after completion of the prototype is thought given to re-purposing the agent. XML has mitigated the problem, but hasn't removed the challenge of layperson authoring. Digital puppets were designed to have an integrated user-friendly authoring environment. We wished to separate the content authoring and the context authoring, and did not want to distract users with low-level animation details. Puppets speak exactly the lines they are authored to speak but their gestures and facial animation are generated automatically from contextual hints; thus, the puppets act with limited autonomy.

2 Related Work

With respect to authoring, animated characters fall into three categories, sequentially scripted characters, limited autonomous characters, and autonomous planning agents. Scriptable online characters such as those from Oddcast, Haptek, Microsoft have become increasingly common in the commercial domain where they act as social interfaces or guides [4][13][21]. Because each utterance and gesture must be specified, and because the associated graphics must be kept simple, these interface aids are of limited general use. More sophisticated commercial applications such as those by Conversive and EDrama apply templates and rules to alleviate repetitiveness and provide a degree of autonomy [9][11]. Whereas commercial applications of animated characters assume simple scripting and graphics, research applications explore multimedia presentation and discourse planning, and the animation of complex behaviors[3][17][10].

Digital puppets are limited autonomous characters. They are scripted and sequenced, much like in AutoTutor 2 [10][22], though the puppet-scripting model allows for greater flexibility, supporting parallel actions, behavior choices and behavior probabilities. The main difference, however, is the use of presentation goals to create autonomous gestures. In this respect our puppet is similar to Andre and Rist's PPP Persona, a multipurpose presentation agent [2][3]. However, puppets do not plan, and thus are not intelligent or autonomous agents. Though they are less powerful within any particular domain, it is fairly efficient to transfer puppets to new domains.

The work presented here is compatible with work on automated behavior expression, especially the BodyChat and BEAT systems [6][7]. In BodyChat, gaze behaviors, for example, are fully automated for turn-taking in multi-participant settings. Though the Digital Puppets' behavioral domain is not social communication per se, some of its behaviors are similarly automated, and could be further developed using BEAT. Gestures signifying attentiveness to user actions, deictic gestures indicating on-screen objects such as lesson pages or simulation interfaces, and idle behaviors such as weight and gaze shifts, blinks and head movements are automated. These automatic behaviors may be overridden by authored behaviors, e.g., those which are attached to content-free initiators and responses, in the case of the tutorial agent, or gestures chosen to accompany presentation material, in the case of the presentation agent.

3   2D Character Creation and Animation

3.1   Graphical Realization

The prototypes for the character animation system were Adele [25], the tutor for our case-based clinical practice training simulation, and Carmen and Gina, characters in the interactive drama, Carmen's Bright Ideas [19], which teaches problem-solving skills to mothers of pediatric cancer patients. Adele uses classic limited animation techniques - 2D sequences of frames that always return to a default position. Adele's persona was rendered directly by an artist using a commercial paint program. Carmen's Bright Ideas uses traditional hand drawn character animation, realized as 2D computer graphics using Macromedia's Flash. The agent-controlled characters, Carmen and Gina, use composite Flash libraries for gestures, head and eye positions, and facial expressions.

The 2D behavior-library approach is useful in a number of contexts. Many agent domains are limited in their requirements for visual behavior, relying on synthetic speech to provide necessary depth and breadth. Applications that use a 2D interface look flat in the context of a 3D character, and real time rendering to line-and-fill art is technically challenging. The limited-animation, 2D cartoon character as the basis for a persona seems useful and viable for pedagogical applications, particularly for young learners. Such libraries are most useful when we can load and unload components as needed. In the case of hand-drawn art, if the agent's domain changes, or requires additional behaviors, the same artist must be re-engaged, and spend many more hours in the labor intensive task of hand drawing the new frames.

Research budgets and circumstances make this approach less than ideal. To make our 2D personas feasible, we opted for a *build-once, use-forever* production path. The character for the first Digital Puppet system, Skip, was built using Alias Wavefront's Maya, a commercial 3D animation program. Any competent character animator can create new behaviors for Skip, and rendered output will always match the original art, so libraries of behavior can be built up over time. In addition, a procedural system such as Maya allows for the generalization of behaviors across characters.

To maximize behavioral capability, we render and animate the character in layers, allowing us to achieve independent control of important features. Eyes, brows, mouth and body can each be rendered separately so that the character can raise its brows while speaking, speak while gesturing, shift its gaze and weight when attending to user actions, etc. This capability introduces a new problem - registering the 2D layers, in particular, the head and body. In 3D, as the gesticulating body rotates around, the 2D perspective projection of the head-body registration point changes. In 2D, the separately-rendered head positions remain stationary. Because the camera is fixed for all animations, we determine a projection matrix, apply it to the 3D registration point, and then compute a translation that aligns the 2D registration point on the head with the one on the body.

3.2 Creating Behaviors

Behaviors can thus be created to meet the evolving needs of the agent. We begin with a basic library that makes the character come alive: weight and gaze shifts, saccades, blinks and head movements. In the case of the presentation agent, Skip, behaviors specific to expository speaking and the use of visual aids are added on top of these. Maya animation sequences are created and rendered by Cambridge Animation System's Swiffworks shader at base body orientations (e.g., toward the user, toward the screen) to Macromedia's Flash format, which provides indexing and editing capabilities. For additional flexibility, we use scalable vector graphics (SVG) as our target display format. This allows us to scale the images to the optimal size for the screen layout and employ a variety of cameras, from full body shots for gestures to closeups for conversational behaviors. To avoid the latency currently associated with parsing a document object model, we convert the final SVG files to the portable network graphics format, gaining speed but losing the ability to further scale animations.

Beyond the basic behavior library, the animators must create behaviors related to a particular domain that will be used by the character. We collected and studied video footage of human presenters, and human tutors working with users of computer applications. The reference footage permits the animators to anticipate what kinds of moves will be indispensable. In the presentation domain deictic gestures combined with beats are the most common gestures. Deictics are easy to define procedurally and generically useful. Future additions to a presentation puppet might include tutorial gestures related to orienting the user and using the application interface.

The image libraries are loaded into the puppet animation engine. XML descriptions of gestures, comprised of sequenced and procedural frames, are generated by a graphical animation editing tool. Table 1 shows the output of the editor. Background animations are performed automatically when the engine is idling, and sending a text string automatically results in lip synced text-to-speech synthesis at any of several different head positions.

4 Animation Authoring

Digital puppets require several types of input: Users must supply text for the puppet to speak and environments must supply contextual hints that enables an inferencing module to select appropriate behaviors. The selection is informed by video analysis, presentation techniques [1], and facial communication displays

Table 1. A viseme sequence and a body gesture example in Widget.xml.

```
⟨head⟩
    ⟨!-- Frames for viseme sequence for position 000 --⟩
    ⟨frame filename="head/head-000-phonemes{0001..0012}.svgz"⟩
        ⟨mount name="body" coordinate="0, 25.632, 0.351" /⟩
    ⟨/frame⟩ ...
⟨/head⟩
⟨body⟩
    ⟨!-- Frames for body gesture weight shift --⟩
    ⟨gesture name="weight-shift"⟩
        ⟨sequence subtype="middle-to-left-to-right"
            progression="weight-shift0001..0009" /⟩
    ⟨/gesture⟩
⟨/body⟩
```

[8]. Based on the input, the inferencing module generates a runtime script and sends it to the animation engine for display.

We use contextual hints to select behaviors in two ways. In every domain, there are naturally occurring high-concept goals. For example, in the presentation domain there are the components of the presentation task, *introduce, explain, etc.* and in the tutoring domain there is the flow of the application task. The markup for scripting the puppet's behavior at this level is shown in Table 2. The *PreIntro* is the initial context; in this state the camera might zoom in and the puppet might look around and speak. When the viewer begins the presentation, the puppet moves to the *Introduction* state, which specifies that the puppet first glance at the button, and then orient itself with its body facing toward the viewer before speaking. There are idle and end states as well. A type of *choices* will choose one [group] of the gestures, while a type of *gspeak* will specify a facial animation or gesture to perform while speaking.

The more interesting mapping of behaviors occurs at lower levels, where gestures are mapped to contexts and goals, for example, *elaborate* in the presentation domain and *increase politeness* in the tutoring domain, as well as to sentence fragments, words, and patterns, such as exclamations and numbers. This intention-based mapping is similar to the approach of Andre and Rist [3], who use presentation goals to select their animation schema. A gesture is executed randomly and probabilistically after the sentence starts. Several examples are shown in Table 3.

The animation engine executes the script commands asynchronously and in parallel, depending on the command. The script uses a special-purpose XML schema that is narrowly defined for digital puppets and was not created as a general standard. Though the 2D puppet schema is compatible with other standards, most animation languages – Affective Presentation Markup Language(APML), Multimodal Utterance Representation Markup Language (MURML), Rich Representation Language(RRL), Virtual Human Markup Language(VHML) – control 3D avatar movement and communication in virtual environments. Similarly, there are 3D facial animation standards that focus on realistic control.

Table 2. The mapping of high-level contextual information to gestures.

```
⟨context name=PreIntro⟩
    ⟨s type=camera name=closer⟩                  ⟨context name=Intro⟩
    ⟨s type=gspeak text="Come {%talkGesture           ⟨s type=turnhead
        :default%} in and sit down."⟩                       to=044 wait=true⟩
    ⟨s type=wait for=second value=5⟩              ⟨s type=wait
    ⟨s type=gspeak text="We {%turnhead:044%}             for=second value=1⟩
        are waiting for people to arrive."⟩      ⟨s type=turnhead
    ⟨s type=choices⟩                                     to=000 wait=true⟩
        ⟨c type=pose gesture=talkGesture         ⟨s type=turnbody
            subtype=default⟩                            to=000 wait=true⟩
        ⟨c type=nothing⟩                          ⟨insert_point⟩
        ⟨c type=group⟩
            ⟨g type=turnhead to=044 wait=true⟩   insert authored text
            ⟨g type=turnhead to=000 wait=true⟩
        ⟨/c⟩
    ⟨/s⟩                                          ⟨/insert_point⟩
    ⟨s type=wait for=second value=5⟩             ⟨/context⟩
    ⟨s type=jump context=PreIntro⟩
⟨/context⟩
```

Table 3. The mapping of low-level text and contextual information to gestures.

```
⟨word⟩
    ⟨entry word = "this"                         ⟨context⟩
        gesture = "lifthandpoint"                    ⟨entry context = "Introduction"
        subtype = "default"                              gesture = "talkgesture1"
        probability = "100" /⟩                           subtype = "default"
    ⟨entry word = "but|but,"                              probability = "50"
        gesture = "shiftweightright"                 /⟩
        subtype = "default"                      ⟨/context⟩
        probability = "50" /⟩                    ⟨goal⟩
⟨/word⟩                                              ⟨entry goal = "clain"
⟨sentence⟩                                               gesture = "lookaround"
    ⟨entry fragment = "in fact"                          subtype = "default"
        gesture = "talkgesture"                          probability = "50"
        subtype = "default"                          /⟩
        probability = "100" /⟩                   ⟨/goal⟩
⟨/sentence⟩
```

5   Puppet Applications

5.1   Puppets for Developing Oral Presentation Skills

Digital puppets were created as part of an application to teach fourth and fifth grade students how to construct oral presentations. The goal of the project was to improve science learning through the use of digital puppets in peer teaching and collaborative learning settings. Because of the user base, a user-friendly WYSIWYG puppet authoring tool, shown in Figure 1 on the left, was developed in parallel with the animation engine, instead of as an afterthought. The tool enables users to annotate Web pages and use the annotations to generate commentary and animation.

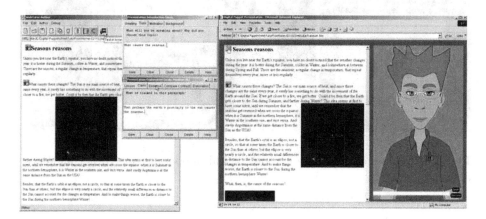

Fig. 1. On the left is the WYSIWYG presentation authoring tool with a Web page and two authoring boxes displayed. On the right is the resulting browser-based puppet presentation. Interactive buttons have been inserted in the Web page.

Our approach to authoring the puppets was based on Rhetorical Structure Theory (RST) [18] and then generalized to accommodate any presentation goal. By constraining the domain, we can reasonably infer the intent of the author with respect to the authored commentary. For example, in the introduction, a user must provide text to motivate the topic. Based on the context and goal, the inferencing module might select behaviors appropriate to motivation and introductions, such as face viewer, perform inviting gesture, and amplify voice.

Figure 1, left, shows the digital puppet user authoring tool, which contains a Web page about the topic to be presented. Clicking on a paragraph of text brings up a small authoring windows, shown at center, that displays the particular concepts that the students must address in their explanations. These goals (e.g., *lesson, claim, evidence*) can be tailored for different contexts (i.e., *introduction, explanation, and conclusion.*) Students provide an introduction, a conclusion and several paragraph-linked explanations that, when played together, will result in an oral presentation about the subject matter. The user publishes the resulting puppet-enhanced Web page by clicking on a button. The published page contains the presentation text (authored input) and contextual hints (presentation goals), the HTML-based puppet commands and interactive buttons, and the JavaScript-based puppet control engine. The Web page and Java-based puppet applet are automatically displayed in adjacent browser frames, as shown in Figure 1 and Figure 2. The user activates the presentation by pressing the interactive buttons.

Fig. 2. Skip gives a presentation about digital puppets at an AIED conference event.

5.2   Wizard of Oz Study for Socially Intelligent Agents Project

Digital puppets are also being used in a wizard of oz study as part of a research project on socially intelligent agents (SIAgents) in educational domains, to assess the appropriateness of the output of a dialogue generator. In this study, a domain expert watches a student perform a task within the Virtual Factory Teaching System, an educational factory modeling application and simulation to teach undergraduate engineering students production and inventory management. (See Figure 3.) If the expert chooses to initiate a speech act, in order to comment or give advice, he selects an appropriate topic and politeness level from the expert interface and an utterance is generated and sent to the user.

As in the presentation system, the generated text is sent verbatim to the puppet. To generate the animation requires contextual information that allows us to map behaviors to textual input. The SIAgents system is based on the Politeness Theory of Brown and Levinson [5], and uses that model to influence the student's motivational state. The system has a rich user model, which influences the generated dialogue. For example, if the system determines that a user is frustrated, it can initiate dialogue to mitigate a face threat. The politeness factor was therefore used as a context for mapping behaviors. The system also has an extensive plan, and can tell if user is deep in a task, or only beginning or concluding one. The plan provides another context within which to script behaviors. The model is extensible, so that one can use as much or as little context as required to influence a puppet's animation behaviors.

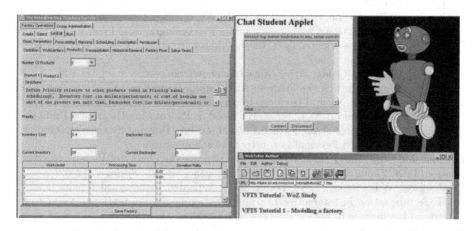

Fig. 3. Widget tutors a student using the the Virtual Factory Teaching System.

6   Conclusion

Digital puppets have potential as online commentators and presenters because they combine ease of authoring and automated behavior generation, allowing novice users to build characters that can act with limited autonomy within their particular domains. By generating 2D puppets from 3D characters, we can quickly create new animations and build up libraries of behavior. We have deployed two different characters in two different environments - presentation and tutorial - and have found the process of moving to a new domain to be fairly efficient. As computing power increases and characters can be animimated more quickly, believability will improve and conversational interfaces will become an interface standard. Because reasoning in complex domains will remain a hard problem for much time to come, we expect limited autonomous agents such as the digital puppet to bridge the gap between narrators and intelligent tutors.

References

1. Gross Davis, B.: Tools for Teaching. Jossey-Bass. (1993)
2. André, E.: The Generation of Multimedia Presentations. (1982)
3. André, E., Rist, T., Müller, J.: Integrating reactive and scripted behaviors in life-like presentation agents. In K.P. Sycara and M. Wooldridge (Eds.), *Proc. of the Second Int'l Conf. on Autonomous Agents* pp. 261-268, ACM Press, New York. (1998)

4. Ball, L.: Lifelike computer characters: The persona project at Microsoft (1996)
5. Brown, P., Levinson, C.: Politeness: Some universals in language use. New York: Cambridge University Press. (1987)
6. Cassell, J., Vilhjlmsson, H.: Fully Embodied Conversational Avatars: Making Communicative Behaviors Autonomous. Autonomous Agents and Multi-Agent Systems 2(1): 45-64. (1999)
7. Cassell, J., Vilhjalmsson, H., Bickmore, T.: BEAT: the Behavior Expression Animation Toolkit. SIGGRAPH Computer Graphics Proceedings, AMC Press (2001)
8. Chovil, N.: Discourse-oriented facial displays in conversation. Research on Language and Social Interaction. (1991)
9. Conversive: InstantAgents, http://www.conversive.com
10. Drumwright, E. Putting the Sizzle in AutoTutor2. Report.
11. EDrama Learning: Natural language in simulated conversation. (2002)
12. Ganeshan, R., Johnson, W.L, Shaw, E., Wood, B.P.: Tutoring Diagnostic Problem Solving. In Proceedings of the Fifth Int'l Conf. on Int. Tutoring Systems. (2000)
13. Haptek: Automated Personalities, http://www.haptek.com
14. Johnson, W.L.: Using agent technology to improve the quality of Web-based education. In N. Zhong & J. Liu (Eds.) Web Intelligence. Berlin: Springer. (2002)
15. Johnson, W.L., Rickel, J.W., Lester, J.C.: Animated Pedagogical Agents: Face-to-Face Interaction in Interactive Learning Environments. International Journal of Artificial Intelligence in Education 11, 47-78. (2000)
16. Lepper, M.R., Henderlong, J.: Turning "play" into "work" and "work" into "play": 25 years of research in intrinsic versus extrinsic motivation. In C. Sansone & J.M. Harackiewicz (Eds.), Intrinsic and Extrinsic Motivation: The Search for Optimal Motivation and Performance, pp. 257-307. San Diego: Academic Press. (2000)
17. Lester, J.C., Converse, S.A., Kahler, S.E., Barlow, S.T., Stone, B.A., Bhogal, R.S.: The persona effect: Affective impact of animated pedagogical agents. In Proceedings of CHI '97, 359-366. (1997)
18. Mann, W.C., Thompson, S.A.: Rhetorical structure theory: A theory of text organization. Technical Report ISI/RS-87-190, ISI, Univ. of Southern Cal. (1987)
19. Marsella, S., Johnson, W.L., LaBore, C.M.: Interactive Pedagogical Drama. In Proceedings of the 4th Int'l Conference on Autonomous Agents, Agents 2000
20. Marsella, S., Johnson, W.L., LaBore, C.M.: Interactive Pedagogical Drama for Health Interventions. In 11th Int'l Conf. on AI in Education. (2003)
21. Oddcast: SitePal, http://vhost.oddcast.com (1996)
22. Person, N.K., Craig, S., Price, P., Hu, X., Gholson, B., Graesser, A.C., and the Tutoring Research Group: Incorporating Human-like Conversational Behaviors into AutoTutor. IUI (2003)
23. Reeves, B. and Nass, C.: The media equation. Cambridge University Press. (1996)
24. Shaw, E., Ganeshan, R., Johnson, W.L., Millar, D.: Building a case for agent-assisted learning as a catalyst for curriculum reform in medical education. In Proceedings of the Ninth Int'l Conf. on AI in Education. IOS Press. (1999)
25. Shaw, E., Johnson, W.L., Ganeshan, R.: Pedagogical agents on the Web. In Proceedings of the Third International Conference on Autonomous Agents. (1999)
26. Stone, Lester: Dynamically sequencing an animated pedagogical agent. (1996)
27. Rist, T., André, E., and Múller, J.: Adding Animated Presentation Agents to the Inter-face. In Proceedings of the 1997 International Conference On Intelligent User Interfaces, pages 79-86, Orlando, Florida. (1997)
28. Rizzo, P., Shaw, E., Johnson, W.L.: An Agent that Helps Children to Author Rhetorically-Structured Digital Puppet Presentations. In Proceedings of ITS. (2002)

Non-photorealistic 3-D Facial Animation on the PDA Based on Facial Expression Recognition

Soo-Mi Choi[1], Yong-Guk Kim[1*], Don-Soo Lee[1], Sung-Oh Lee[2] and Gwi-Tae Park[2]

[1] School of Computer Engineering, Sejong University, Seoul, Korea
{smchoi, ykim*}@sejong.ac.kr
[2] Department of Electrical Engineering, Korea University, Seoul, Korea

Abstract. This paper presents a facial expression recognition-synthesis system. In the front, it detects a facial area within the given image and then classifies its facial expression into 7 emotional weightings. Such weighting information, transmitted to the PDA via a mobile network, is used for non-photorealistic facial expression animation. The cartoon-like shading method, adopted as a non-photorealistic 3-D technique, is developed to render a 3-D avatar that conveys a familiar and yet unique facial character, even without employing extensive polygons. We found that facial expression animation using emotional curves is more effective in expressing the timing of an expression comparing to the linear interpolation method. The present emotional avatar embedded on a mobile platform can be used in the cyberspace.

1 Introduction

We identify someone by looking at his face, since each person typically has unique and distinctive features in the face. Moreover, human face is a great communication device, because the face can evoke diverse facial expressions according to the internal emotions. So one can read someone's emotional state from his facial expression and respond to it appropriately.

Although the study on facial expression has a rather long history since Charles Darwin, automatic analysis of human facial expressions using the computer is a recent trend [3,5]. It is known that there are six basic (or prototypical) facial expressions for humans across the diverse ethnicities and cultures: happiness, surprise, sadness, fear, anger and disgust [2,8]. Our present study is also based upon this assumption and deals with such cases.

Humans are able to recognize facial expressions of the rendered face on the screen (or paper) as well as of the real face. In fact, researchers in the computer graphics and multimedia areas have been developed a series of face models and their implementations for using in diverse human-computer interaction applications or for animating an avatar in the cyberspace. As an example, the early attempt of unifying the facial expression recognition and facial animation envisioned such virtual face avatar as a future communication media [6].

The present study will present a multi-step pipeline: in the first step the facial expressions of the face within the video images are recognized as a time sequence; in

A. Butz et al. (Eds.): SG 2004, LNCS 3031, pp. 11-20, 2004.
© Springer-Verlag Berlin Heidelberg 2004

the second step the extracted emotional information is transmitted to a remote client via the mobile network; in the final step the cartoon-like 3-D facial expressions are rendered on a PDA using that information.

Despite the fact that the PDA (and smart-phone) become widespread because of its mobility and convenience as the post-PC systems, its processing power for rendering the 3-D animation is yet limited. To circumvent such shortcoming, we have designed a non-realistic 3-D model that does not need many polygons in drawing a face.

The structure of the paper is as follow. In section 2, we illustrate the overall system. The processes of automatic recognition of facial expressions will be described in section 3. In section 4, we show how to animate the facial expressions. Experimental results and conclusions will be presented in section 5.

2   Overview

Fig. 1 illustrates the overall structure of our system, which consists of two main parts. The first part is to classify the facial expressions of the video image acquired using a camera attached to the PC. To classify the facial expression, it needs to detect the facial area within the given image and then to normalize the selected facial area according to a template. The facial expression information obtained at the first part is transmitted to the next part via the mobile network. The computing platform of the second part is a mobile PDA, which has Internet connection and yet has limited processing power and memory size. We have adopted a non-photorealistic method in rendering a 3-D facial expression on the PDA.

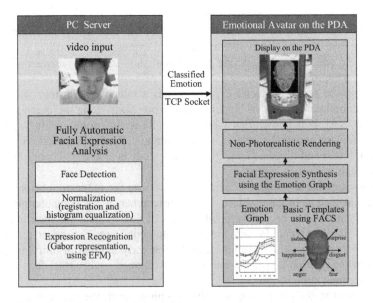

Fig. 1. The schematic diagram of the facial expression recognition-synthesis system.

3 Automatic Facial Expression Recognition

In general, the facial expression recognition system consists of three stages: in the first stage, it detects a face area within the given image, called the face detection; in the second stage, the positions of three facial features (i.e. two eyes and mouth) will be located within the detected face for normalizing the face area; the final stage classifies a facial expression of the given face using a classifier.

In our study, SVM (Support Vector Machine), a supervised neural network developed on a powerful statistical learning technique [9], is used for the face detection task, by training it using, for example, face images and non-face image as shown in Fig. 2(a) by interleaving them. In addition, it is possible to train the SVM that is also able to deal with size variation and rotation of the face. In any case, once a face is detected using this machine, the face image needs to be normalized by locating the positions of two eyes and the mouth. The SVM method is used for this task as well. Note that the location of the mouth is included for the present case, which contrasts to the face perception case where only the locations of two eyes are typically used for normalization [5].

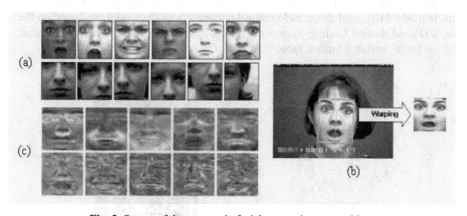

Fig. 2. Stages of the automatic facial expression recognition.

Fig. 2(b) illustrates a warping operation as a normalization process. Our previous study suggests that such normalization is a crucial stage that could impact upon the overall performance of the facial expression recognition system [5]. After the normalization stage, Gabor wavelets are applied to the 20X20 grid drawn over the image, and the convolution output from this operation is forwarded to the next stage to classify the facial expression. For this purpose, we have used the EFM (Enhanced Fisher Discriminant Model), which in fact combines PCA (Principal Component Analysis) with Fisher Discriminant, and it was initially developed for the face perception. The top row of Fig. 2(c) shows the first five PCA components of the given image and the bottom row the EFM components, respectively. Comparative study shows that performance of the system has increased by adding Gabor wavelets at least 10% and the EFM outperforms the PCA. When the Gabor wavelets and the EFM are combined, the recognition rate of the system reaches to 92%.

4   Non-photorealistic 3-D Facial Animation on the PDA

In this section, we describe about the present facial animation that preserves the timing of facial expression according to the emotional curves obtained by the automatic facial expression recognition system. In order to increases the speed of animation on the PDA without using a 3-D graphics accelerator, we have developed a simple muscle-based 3-D face model which contains less extensive number of polygons. Moreover, a non-photorealistic rendering technique is applied to the model to enhance familiarity and uniqueness of the 3-D faces.

4.1 A Simple Muscle-Based 3-D Face Model

Facial animation on a PDA using the base key-model begins with a neutral expression. The base key-model has polygonal structure that makes the face deformable based upon a muscle model. To increase the speed, the number of vertices and polygons is reduced except for the expressive regions such as two eyes, the mouth and the nose. The muscle movements for animating a 3-D face are mainly based on Waters' linear muscle model [10]. And the muscle control parameters in the model are based on the FACS (Facial Action Coding System)[2, 12], which can describe all possible basic 'Action Units' within a human face.

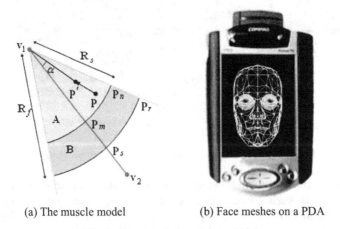

(a) The muscle model   (b) Face meshes on a PDA

Fig. 3. The muscle-based face model.

Fig. 3(a) illustrates the linear muscle model and Fig. 3(b) shows the face meshes, respectively. A muscle is modeled as the vector that has a direction from the point of bone v_1 to the point of skin v_2. It is assumed that there is no displacement at the bony attachment and maximum deflection occurs at the point of the skin. The extension of vector field is described by cosine functions and fall off factors that has a cone shape. A dissipation of the force is passed to the adjoining tissue from the sector **A** to **B** as illustrated in Fig. 3 (a). R_s and R_f represent the fall-off radius start and its finish, respectively. The new displacement $\mathbf{p}'$ of an arbitrary vertex $\mathbf{p}$ within the zone $(\mathbf{v}_1, \mathbf{p}_r, \mathbf{p}_s)$ is computed as follows:

$$\mathbf{p}' = \mathbf{p} + \cos(\alpha)\, kr\, (\mathbf{p}\mathbf{v}_1 / \|\mathbf{p}\mathbf{v}_1\|) \tag{1}$$

where α is the angle between the vectors $(\mathbf{v}_1, \mathbf{v}_2)$ and $(\mathbf{v}_1, \mathbf{p})$, $\mathbf{D}$ is $\|\mathbf{v}_1 - \mathbf{p}\|$, k is a fixed constant representing the elasticity of skin, and r is the radial displacement parameter:

$$r = \begin{cases} \cos(1 - \mathbf{D}/\mathbf{R}_s) & \text{for } \mathbf{p} \text{ inside zone } (\mathbf{v}_1, \mathbf{p}_n, \mathbf{p}_m) \\ \cos((\mathbf{D} - \mathbf{R}_s)/(\mathbf{R}_f - \mathbf{R}_s)) & \text{for } \mathbf{p} \text{ inside zone } (\mathbf{p}_n, \mathbf{p}_r, \mathbf{p}_s, \mathbf{p}_m) \end{cases} \tag{2}$$

The complexity of the algorithm depends on the number of vertices it has to check to see whether they are inside the zone of influence as shown in Fig. 3(a). The linear muscle model is useful for a 3-D face model that has a small number of polygons [7]. As shown in Fig. 3(b), the present base key-model contains only 762 vertices and 476 polygons. Among them, 474 vertices and 296 polygons are allocated for rendering the whole face, and 288 vertices and 180 polygons for the eyeball region in particular. The present 3-D face model has been divided into three regions, i.e. the upper, middle and lower parts of the face. Since it is known that a muscle within a sub region of the face will have influence on the others, it is possible to eliminate all the vertices that are outside the region by checking the flags. Opening of the mouth is animated by rotating the vertices of the lower part of the face about a jaw pivot axis. To create a natural oval-looking mouth, the vertices on the lower lip are rotated by different amounts. The upper lip is also affected by the jaw rotation.

4.2 Non-photorealistic Rendering

In general, non-photorealistic graphics refers to a set of techniques for creating images where artistic expression is the immediate goal, rather than adherence to photorealism. In order to add humor and emotional appeal, our system employs cartoon-like shading [1] as a non-photorealistic rendering (NPR) technique, rather than smoothly interpolating shading across a model as in *Gouraud* shading. By reducing the amount of visual details, it is possible to synthesize a 3-D face that conveys a familiar and yet unique facial character, which is useful for exchanging information effectively or for story telling in the cyberspace.

In our system, the diffuse lighting at the vertices is defined by the following lighting equation:

$$C_i = a_g a_m + a_l a_m + (\max\{L \cdot n, 0\})\, d_l d_m \tag{3}$$

C_i is the vertex color, a_g is the coefficient of global ambient light, a_l and d_l are the ambient and diffuse coefficients of the light source, and a_m and d_m are the ambient and diffuse coefficients of the object's material. L is the unit vector from the light source to the vertex, and n is the unit normal to the surface at the vertex. Instead of calculating the colors per vertex, a 1-D texture map of a minimal number of colors is computed and stored ahead of time (i.e. illuminated main color, shadow color, and highlight color--See Fig. 4(a)). The main color of the texture map is calculated by replacing the dot product term in Equation (3) with a value of one. The shadow color is calculated by replacing the dot product term with a value of zero. The color of the highlight is determined by multiplying the material color by a highlight factor. Fig. 4(b) demonstrates six emotional key-models corresponding to specific facial expressions based on the FACS. For example, action units for surprise expression are inner brow raiser, outer brow raiser, and jaw drop.

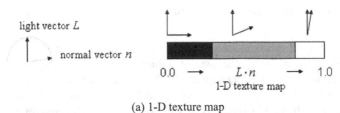

(a) 1-D texture map

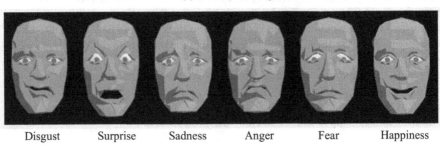

| Disgust | Surprise | Sadness | Anger | Fear | Happiness |

(b) Six basic expressions created by non-photorealistic rendering

Fig. 4. 1-D texture map and six basic expressions.

4.3 Non-linear Expression Interpolation Based on the Emotional Curves

Combining of key expression poses and interpolation is probably the most widely used technique for implementing and controlling facial animation. Given the starting expression pose E_1 and the final expression pose E_2, an intermediate pose is generated by a fractional interpolation coefficient α.

$$E = \alpha E_1 + (1-\alpha)E_2 \quad 0.0 < \alpha < 1.0 \tag{4}$$

Generally, we manipulate the interpolation coefficient as a function of animation frame time. The linear interpolation seems smooth because it moves each surface point a small equal distance in successive frames. However, facial motions are not linear but tend to accelerate and decelerate. For example, surprise is perhaps the briefest expression and sadness is often prolonged in duration.

Fig. 5 shows the seven emotional curves (i.e. neutral, surprise, fear, sadness, anger, disgust, happiness) obtained by automatic facial expression recognition. The emotional curves give weighting information for facial synthesis. The horizontal axis shows the change of time and the vertical one represents the similarity measure. The separation between surprise curve and the other ones indicate that facial expression is changed neutral into surprise at time 7.

As the basis for generating non-linear expression synthesis, we use the concepts of weighting information based on emotional curves and blending functions. Each emotion has an emotional curve obtained by automatic facial expression recognition. Each emotional expression also has an associated target set of facial control parameter values. The actual parameter value used at a given animation frame time $F_p(t)$ is determined by blending emotional curves using a weighted average:

$$F_p(t) = \sum_{e=1}^{n}(W_{ep}(t)T_{ep})/\sum_{e=1}^{n}W_{ep}(t) \qquad (5)$$

where n is the number of recognized expressions and T_{ep} are the target facial control parameter values. W_{ep} is the weight of an emotional expression. For stable animation, two dominant expressions are blended in runtime.

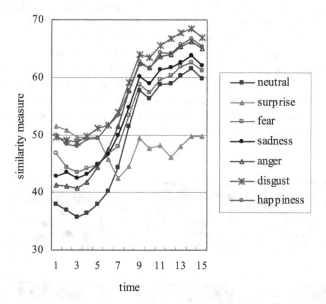

Fig. 5. Emotional curves obtained by the facial expression recognition system.

5   Implementation and Results

Fig. 6 shows six basic facial expressions of a subject from the standard Cohn-Kanade database [3], and the corresponding emotional similarity measurements for each facial image are shown as a bar graph beside each image. In the bar graph, each vertical bar represents the similarity measure to one of the seven emotions from neutral (1), surprise (2), fear (3), sadness (4), anger (5), disgust (6) and happiness (7) from the left to the right, respectively. For instance, as Fig. 6(a) is the image for 'surprise', the height of the bar (2) is the shortest among seven vertical bars, indicating that the measurement by the system agrees with our visual perception.

The PDA used as a client system is an iPAQ 3950 (400MHz, 64Mbytes) from HP, and we have developed the software system using Embedded Visual C++ 3.0 and PocketGL^{TM} as a PocketPC 3-D graphics library. Considering the limitation of processing speed of the PDA, we have used minimum number of polygons in rendering the 3-D face, and have adopted an optimization method for the floating-point operations [4].

The non-photorealistic 3-D faces implemented in the present study are shown in Fig. 7. The relationship between the original faces and the corresponding 3-D faces obtained by emotional curves is illustrated. The input face image is in Fig. 7(a) and Fig. 7(b) and (c) shows the 3-D facial expressions using emotional curves, and (b) and (c) are generated by flat shading and by the cartoon shading, respectively. Although each face contains a small number of polygons, it appears to be smooth and primary facial features such as the mouth and two eyes are distinguished. And, the 3-D face can be seen from different angles including a side view as shown in Fig. 7(c) and (d). The animation sequence by emotional curves is illustrated in Fig. 7(c), while similar sequence by linear interpolation method in Fig. 7(d). When you compare two sequences, it may be able to observe that two eyes and the mouth already attain a certain smiling at the fourth frame in Fig. 7(c), whereas they do not yet in Fig. 7(d). As the recent research suggests that humans are very sensitive on the timing of facial expression, the facial animation based upon emotional curves reflects more effectively user's emotional state in the time sequence.

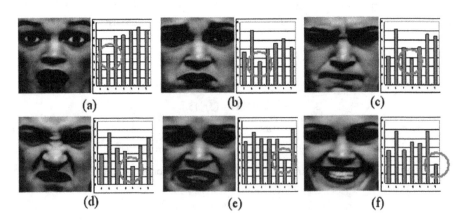

Fig. 6. The results of automatic facial expression recognition.

6 Conclusions and Discussion

The present study demonstrates a pipeline where the facial expression recognition system is integrated with the 3-D facial animation on the PDA via a mobile network. Both automatic analysis of human facial expression and 3-D facial expression animation are still evolving areas [11]. Thus, combining two disciplines has been a nontrivial task. We present a basic framework in which an emotional avatar that attains human emotional states can be generated. In particular, we have found that facial expression synthesis using the emotional curves obtained from the facial expression recognition is more natural in expressing the timing of a facial animation than using the simple linear interpolation method. We have also developed a cartoon shading method as one of the non-photorealistic techniques in rendering an avatar on the PDA without employing extensive polygons.

As many smart phones with a camera are available, and hardware accelerators for 3-D graphics will be included in the near future, it will be possible to exchange messages that contain a 3-D emotional avatar conveying sender's emotional story. This kind of 3-D emotional avatar will obviously replace conventional 2-D emoticons, usually adopted in Internet messenger systems. We expect that this kind of emotional avatar can be an effective communication mean in the ubiquitous computing environment.

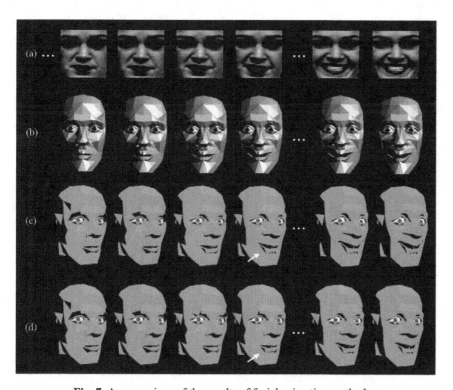

Fig. 7. A comparison of the results of facial animation methods.

References

[1] L. Adam, C. Marshall, M. Harris, and M. Blackstein, "Stylized Rendering Techniques for Scalable Real-Time 3D Animation", In Symposium of Non-Photorealistic Animation and Rendering (NPAR) 2000, pp. 13-20, 2000.

[2] P. Ekman and W. Friesen, *Unmasking the Face. A guide to recognizing emotions from facial clues.* Palo Alto. Consulting Psychologists Press, 1975.

[3] T. Kanade, J. Cohn, and Y. Tian, Comprehensive database for facial expression analysis, Proc. Int'l Conf. Face and Gesture Recognition, pp. 46-53, 2000.

[4] P. Lalonde and R. Dawon, "A High Speed, Low Precision Square Root", Graphics Gems, Academic Press, 1998.

[5] S-H. Lee, Y-G. Kim, and G-T. Park, "Facial Expression Recognition based upon Gabor Wavelets Based Enhanced Fisher Model", LNCS 2869, pp. 490-496, 2003.

[6] N. Magnenat-Thalmann, P. Kalra, and M. Escher, "Face to Virtual face", Proceeding of IEEE, pp.870-883, 1998.

[7] T.D. Bui, D. Heylen, M. Poel, and A. Nijholt, "Exporting Vector Muscles for Facial Animation", Smart Graphics 2003, LNCS 2733, pp. 251-260, 2003.

[8] F.I. Parke and K. Waters, *Computer Facial Animation*, A K Peters, 1996.

[9] V. Vapnik. *Statistical Learning Theory*, John Wiley & Sons, 1998.

[10] K. Waters, "A muscle model for animating three-dimensional facial expressions", SIGGRAPH'87, Vol. 21, pp.17-24, 1987.

[11] I. Buck, A. Finkelstein, C. Jacobs, et al., "Performance-driven hand-drawn animation", In Symposium of Non-Photorealistic Animation and Rendering (NPAR) 2000, pp. 101-108, 2000.

[12] I. Pandzic, R. Forchheimer, *MPEG-4 facial animation – the standard, implementations, and applications*, John Wiley & Sons, 2002.

ALTERNE: Intelligent Virtual Environments for Virtual Reality Art

Marc Cavazza[1], Jean-Luc Lugrin[1], Simon Hartley[1], Paolo Libardi[1],
Matthew J. Barnes[1], Mikael Le Bras[1], Marc Le Renard[2], Louis Bec[3], and Alok Nandi[4]

[1] School of Computing, University of Teesside, Middlesbrough TS1 3BA, United Kingdom
m.o.cavazza@tees.ac.uk
[2] CLARTE, 6 rue Léonard de Vinci, BP 0102, 53001 Laval CEDEX, France
Marc.LeRenard@esiea-ouest.fr
[3] CYPRES, Friche de la Belle de Mai, 41 rue Jobin, 13003, Marseille, France
info@cypres-artech.org
[4] Commediastra, 182, av. W. Churchill, 1180 Brussels, Belgium
nandi@architempo.net

Abstract. Virtual Reality Artworks provide sophisticated user experiences but
their development is a complex process. We describe the use of Intelligent Virtual Environments for VR Art. In this approach, virtual world behaviour is governed by a symbolic system. This supports news forms of experimentation with
physical laws or with causality that we have termed Alternative Reality. In addition, basing world behaviour on a symbolic representation can facilitate collaboration between artists and scientists. We introduce the techniques behind
Alternative Reality and illustrate these with examples from the prototype. We
conclude by an outline of artistic work in progress using these techniques.

1 Introduction

Virtual Reality Art [1] has proven to be one of the most challenging applications of
Virtual Reality (VR). At the same time, artistic installations have provided some of
the most convincing VR experiences. However, the development of VR Art installations is a complex process, even more so considering the necessary collaboration
between artists and scientists. If the artistic creation of virtual worlds is to proceed by
"ways of worldmaking", one natural question is to determine the conceptual level
describing these new worlds. This theoretical question echoes the more pragmatic
one, which seeks to improve the practical collaboration between artists and scientists
in the actual development of VR Art installations. The global framework for this
research is the ALTERNE project, an EU-funded project aiming at developing new
technologies for VR Art, following an Art+Science approach [2]. The project is based
on the concept of Alternative Reality, which revisits the early ideas of VR according
to which its purpose was to provide psychedelic experiences [3] rather than being an
accurate simulation of physical reality.

In the next sections, after a brief presentation of the system's architecture, we describe the technology baseline for Alternative Reality, and how their symbolic nature

A. Butz et al. (Eds.): SG 2004, LNCS 3031, pp. 21-30, 2004.
© Springer-Verlag Berlin Heidelberg 2004

provides a new framework for the collaborative design by artists and scientists. As the artistic work is currently in progress, we conclude by giving a brief outline of how artistic briefs will be making use of this technology.

2 System Overview and Architecture

In order to maximise user experience, Virtual Reality Art is often presented using immersive displays such as CAVEs™. Our target systems are large-scale virtual reality installations, such as the SAS Cube™, which is a 4-wall, PC-based, CAVE™-like, immersive visualisation system. The use of a CAVE™-like system should facilitate interaction with virtual world objects, which is an essential aspect of the alternative reality experience. We achieve this interaction through a game engine, Unreal Tournament 2003™ (UT) that is utilized both as a visualisation engine and as a development environment. Game engines are now increasingly used for visualisation in scientific research due to their rendering performance and their ability to communicate with external software modules [4], which in the present case is essential to the development of a simulation layer that will override basic physics mechanisms. Another interesting aspect is the growing use of game engines for 3D Digital Arts.

In addition, the engine we are using, UT, has previously been ported to CAVE™ systems [5] and we have adapted it to the SAS Cube™, using the original approach described in the CAVE-UT implementation. Figure 1 illustrates the display of one of our test environments in the SAS-Cube™.

This environment supports several interaction mechanisms in terms of object manipulation (which can be grabbed, moved, so as to initiate physical processes), as well as "triggers" that can start certain processes associated with the environment's devices (heating, cooling, flowing, etc.). Game engines such as UT 2003™ include sophisticated behaviour models, which can be broken down into i) event systems that manage user interaction and discretise physical processes and ii) native physics engine supporting realistic simulation. This feature provides an essential path to the implementation of new behavioural layers, which is the technical principle behind the implementation of alternative reality.

3 AI Techniques for World Behaviour

While it is accepted that AI techniques can support virtual agents behaviours, there are fewer applications in which they support the behaviour of the world as a whole, substituting themselves to physical simulation. However, this situation changes dramatically when the objective is to depart from physical realism, i.e. to create alternative worlds obeying different laws of physics. There is a significant history of VR Art creating alternative worlds, such as Osmose™ from Char Davies. Challenging the laws of physics has even been the plot for one of the most popular pieces of animation, The Quarxs™, by Maurice Benayoun. Let us consider the objective of creating alternative worlds in which different laws of physics would apply, or in which causality would be modified. The main conceptual difficulty consists in creating these alternative world behaviour's from a principled basis. Devising mathematical formulations for alternative laws of physics would be highly unpractical, if at all feasible. Rather, physical behaviour could be described at a higher level of abstraction, in terms of the qualitative relations between physical phenomena that constitute physical laws.

There is an obvious advantage in using symbolic descriptions of behaviour. These can be embedded in a knowledge level whose concepts serve as a basis for discussion between artists and scientists. Although this level is not free from formalisation, it is still possible to identify explicit concepts within the AI representations (in the present case, derived from Qualitative physics or Planning) that it uses.

This section describes the fundamental mechanisms developed to describe alternative reality. Their instantiation to actual artistic briefs will be presented in the next section.

Figure 1: Our Test Environments (the Causality Café) in the SAS Cube™.

3.1 Redefining World Behaviour through an Event-Based System

The mechanism underlying the definition of new worlds' behaviours relies on the event system which is associated to the UT engine. This provides a natural discretisation of physical events which supports the overriding of the native physics engine by AI-based behavioural engines. Our architecture is based on an Event Interception System (EIS) that defines specific classes of objects, which can enter a specific event interception mode [6]. In this mode events involving the object (e.g. the object breaking into pieces when being hit) can have their activation delayed. There exists explicit representation for the elementary events (that we refer to as Basic Events), which are low-level events derived from the collision detection mechanisms of the graphic engine, e.g. `Bump(Actor OtherActor)`, `Touch(Actor OtherActor)`, `UnTouch(Actor OtherActor)`, `ActorEnteredVolume(Actor Volume)`, etc. From these basic events, more abstract events are instantiated, by encapsulating the associated representations as well as relevant properties of the objects they involve.

The EIS underlies both the Qualitative Physics Engine and the Causal Engine. In the former case, objects that can take part in qualitative processes intercept physical events involving them so as to allow their behaviour to be under the control of qualitative simulation; basic events are parsed into QP-events that can activate relevant processes. In the latter case, intercepted events can be modified to create causality-inducing event co-occurrences; basic events are parsed into Context Events (CE). For instance, the basic events hit(?obj1, ?obj2) and explode(?obj2) can be encapsulated into a CE_break_object(?obj1, ?obj2). As the explosion effect has been intercepted, the corresponding CE is termed "frozen". This status allows a whole range of transformation prior to its re-activation, which is the basis for the creation of artificial causal impressions.

Finally, basic events are associated animations visualizing their effects. They also constitute the basis for the integration between the discretise event system and the visual effects in the virtual environment.

3.2 From Qualitative Physics to Alternative Physics

Qualitative Physics [7] has been developed for the symbolic simulation of physical processes. We have extended its use to the definition of alternative physical laws, which support the definition of alternative world behaviour on a principled basis. The principle behind qualitative physics is to make discrete the variation of physical properties and to model all physical transformations through processes that encapsulate the relation between physical variables, through the notion of influence equations (see details of process described below). The qualitative physics engine is implemented in an external C++ program that communicates with the UT 3D environment [8].

We can illustrate alternative physics through the definition of a fluid flow process which describes the filling of a glass, which is allowed to contain more fluid than its volume would normally allow:

```
Process: Fluid-flow (?source ?sub ?dst ?path)
Individuals:    ?source a contained liquid
                ?destination a contained liquid
                ?sub a substance
                ?Path a fluid-path
Preconditions: Connects (?path, ?source, ?dst)
               Aligned (?path)
Quantity Conditions:
                A [Pressure(C-S(?sub, liquid, ?source))] > A[Pressure(?dst)]

Relations:      Quantity(flow-rate)
                Flow-rate=Pressure(C-S (?sub, liquid, ?source))-Pressure(?Dst)

Influences:     I+(Amount-of-in (?sub, liquid, ?source),A[flow-rate])
                I-(Amount-of-in (?sub, liquid, ?dst),A[Flow-rate])
```

In our example, the filling process increases the amount of water in the glass due to the existence of a water flow from the tap. However the qualitative equations that govern the progression of mass and volume can be dissociated so that, when a certain landmark value is reached, the glass' mass increases independently of its volume. Eventually a limit point for the glass/container mass will be reached and this will

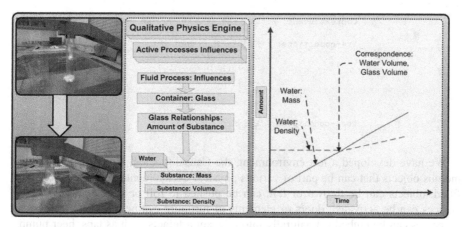

Figure 2: Example of a Qualitative Process in Action: The Alternative "Filling" Process.

determine a new behaviour for the filled glass, such as the glass exploding under the amount of water contained.

Recently, we have extended qualitative modelling to the simulation of physiological systems. In this context, it supports the simulation of life forms, including imaginary ones, which are the subject of the *Arapuca* artistic project (see below).

3.3 Modifying Causality

Causality is an important aspect of how we construct reality. This makes it an ideal target for alternative experiences. There exists several psychological theories aiming at explaining the attribution of causal relations between co-occurring events, starting with Michotte [9]. From an empirical perspective, our objective was to create a system in which the consequences of a given action (generally initiated by the user) could be modified to follow not the "natural" laws of causality but different principles.

The causal engine operates by modifying the Context Events produced by regularly sampling events in the virtual world (which are triggered by processes and/or user intervention). We previously referred to the CEs as "frozen", as their effects are temporarily inhibited. CEs are represented using a STRIPS-like model [10], which makes explicit the pre-condition for the event and its post-conditions in the form of procedural changes to the world. In that representation, there is very much a cause-effect relation between Basic Events detected in the pre-condition and effects triggered in the post conditions.

The basic mechanism for creating "artificial" co-occurrences consists in modifying a CE's post-conditions, after the basic events corresponding to its pre-conditions have been observed. These modifications are performed while the CE is "frozen" through the application of specific Macro-operators (henceforth MOps), which are applied to the STRIPS-like representation of CEs.

```
Context Event: Break_Fragile_Object (?Ob ?Ag)

Pre-conditions: [ BE_Hit(?Ob, ?Ag) ∧
                  Object(?Ob) ∧
                  Object(?Ag) ∧
                  Rigid_Solid_Fragile(?Ob) ∧
                  Rigid_Solid(?Ag) ∧
                  Harder(?Ob,?Ag) ]

Post-conditions: [EFF_Explode(?Ob, ?Ag) ]
```

We have developed a test environment, the Causality Café, which includes a numerous objects that can be part of various physical events (containers can be open or filled, objects can be thrown or fall, can be pushed to roll or slide, can be broken, devices can be activated, doors or elements of furniture can be open, etc.). Physical processes can be embedded naturally into relevant artefacts such as taps, beer pumps and a pool table. For the example we describe here we've been using 58 object instances from 11 object categories (e.g. container, divider) and 9 types of effects (i.e. Break, Bounce, Tilt). The starting event is the user throwing a bottle to the glass door of a refrigerator containing similar bottles. The normal (expected) effect would be for the thrown bottle to break on impact and/or the fridge door itself to break.

The first step when the causal engine receives the "Break_Fragile_Object" CE from the EIS is to determine the best candidate transformations. Among the transformations considered to generate alternative effects are the substitution of the CE's objects (which would result in different objects being broken than the one which was hit) and the propagation of the CE's effects to other objects. Every MOp uses semantic compatibility measures to produce a heuristic value from objects comparisons, effects comparisons and to check the applicability of alternative effects on the CE's objects. One such effect is the propagation of the "break" effect to beer bottles *inside* the fridge, of the same kind as the original (i.e. throwing a bottle at the fridge would break bottles inside it without breaking the fridge's door or penetrating the fridge, see Figure 3). The search process can produce a whole range of alternatives (Figure 3), such as another exploding that the one being hit by the bottle.

More importantly, the strategies for creating such co-occurrences can be controlled using specific types of MOp (for instance, based on analogy). The use of such concepts to direct the strategy is also a basis for discussion between artists and scientists.

4 Example Briefs

In this section we give a brief outline of artistic work in progress which takes advantage of the concept of alternative reality.

4.1 *Arapuca*: Artificial Life Forms in Artificial Ecosystems

This briefs revisits previous work in Digital Arts and Artificial Life [11] with the new tools provided by the ALTERNE approach. It supports the real-time simulation of

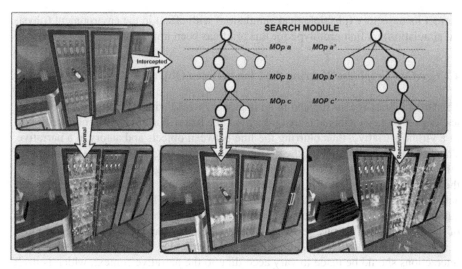

Figure 3. The Causal Engine in Action (see text).

alternative life forms (the Upokrinomena; in our case the specimen is a Diaphapla-nomena) by grounding their behaviour on a model of their internal physiological processes, which is based on Qualitative Physiology. Physical processes in the environment in which the creature evolves (e.g. heat transfer, currents, turbulences, etc.) are also modelled using qualitative physics, hence resulting in the simulation of a complete imaginary ecosystem. Dynamic interactions between the Diaphaplanomena in its environment (such as the creature entering a cold current or being hit by turbulence) generate events that are passed to the simulation engine and alter the current simulation. For instance (Figure 4), if the creature is hit by a turbulence, its course will be modified (physical simulation), which will prompt the Diaphaplanomena to

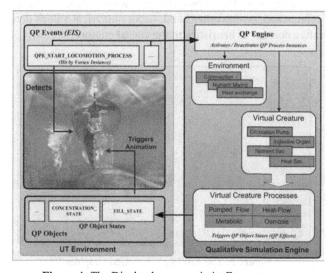

Figure 4: The Diaphaplanomena in its Ecosystem.

correct its trajectory (physiological simulation) with effect in the environment (physical simulation). A first prototype for this brief has been implemented.

4.2 *Ego.Geo Graphies*: **Blurring the Line between Objects and Actors**

This artistic brief is also situated in an imaginary world with alternative laws of physics. One of its key elements is that it features the behaviour of physical objects as part of a virtual narrative, thus blurring the line between objects and actors in a narrative. This brief is an exploration of the notion of context through the variable behaviour of virtual actors and the environment as an actor, responding to the user involvement in the environment. As Figure 5 illustrates, this brief features a certain number of object-actors being emitted by certain areas of the landscape. These acquire the status of autonomous agents, whose main interaction mode with other agents (or with elements of the virtual world) is physical collision. On the other hand, these episodes of interaction are determined by artistic authoring: in particular, the consequences of these interactions should be made to vary according to the narrative context, which is itself influenced by user interaction. Having introduced these elements, we can now relate this brief to our alternative causality system, especially considering the role of collisions and their consequences, which have previously served to illustrate the basic mechanisms of our causal engine. In this brief the effects of collisions will be governed by several high-level factors such as the "empathy" demonstrated by the user towards certain object-actors. In reference to the above described mechanisms, the effects can consist in actors bouncing from obstacles, exploding, or being absorbed by them. In other cases, both colliding entities can disappear creating other objects such as vortices instead. Each collision will thus be associated a set of Context Events, whose post-conditions will be transformed by MOp determined by the current context. In other words, artistic concepts such as empathy, measured for instance by the extent of interaction with certain object categories, will govern causality, through the MOp selection process. The knowledge engineering process consists in identifying possible effects and, on the other hand, using numerical values derived from elements of narrative context as heuristics in the causal engine.

Figure 5: The World of "Ego.Geo Graphies".

As such, the brief is highly relevant to the notion of Intelligent Virtual Environment since the behaviour of the environment as a whole acquires narrative status. This brief is largely under development at the present time. Figure 5 shows an overview of the brief's environment and some of its objects-characters

5 Conclusions and Perspectives

VR Art, in its pursuit of imaginary worlds, raises interesting challenges for Virtual Reality Systems. In particular, the possibility of authoring world behaviour at a conceptual level is a major benefit that can be derived from Intelligent Virtual Environments. Our alternative reality approach introduces two AI-based behavioural techniques, one derived from Qualitative Physics and one inspired from planning techniques. This approach does not solve *per se* the difficult problem of developing software systems from artistic ideas. Rather, in line with its recourse to AI techniques, it takes steps to transform the software development process into a knowledge engineering approach. In that sense, while the direct manipulation of its formalisms by the artists is not a practical proposal, this approach facilitates discussion at a conceptual level, which is closer to the artistic ideas (Figure 6).

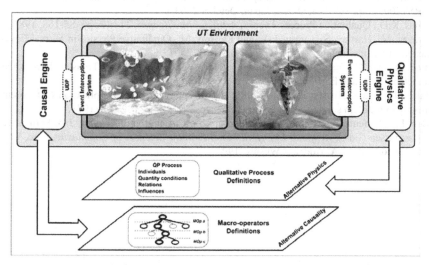

Figure 6. The Representational Layer Underlying Alternative Reality Worlds.

At the same time, the conversion of such ideas into actual world behaviours is also facilitated and this enables fast prototyping and its correlate, quick feedback. Examples of this are for instance: i) the description of alternative laws of physics in plain English, which can then be converted into modification of qualitative processes and ii) the description of causal associations (co-occurrences between categories of events), which can be translated into corresponding search strategies in the causal engine on the basis of high-level concepts such as analogy.

Acknowledgements

The ALTERNE project (IST-38575) is funded in part by the European Commission, under the IST initiative (Cross-Programme Action 15). Sean Crooks is thanked for developing the visuals of Figure 5. Jeffrey Jacobson developed the original CAVE-UT2003 system and is thanked for his assistance in adapting it to the SAS-Cube™.

References

1. Moser, M.A. (Ed.), *Immersed in Technology: Art and Virtual Environments*, Cambridge (Massachussets), MIT Press., 1996.
2. C. Sommerer and L. Mignonneau (Eds.), *Art @ Science*, New York: Springer Verlag, 1998.
3. Leary, T. Chaos and Cyberculture, Ronin Press, 1994.
4. Lewis, M and Jacobson, Games Engines in Scientific Research. *Communications of ACM*, Vol. 45, No. I, pp. 27-31, 2002.
5. Jacobson, J. and Hwang, Z. Unreal Tournament for Immersive Interactive Theater. *Communications of the ACM*, Vol. 45, 1, pp. 39-42, 2002.
6. Cavazza, M., Hartley, S., Lugrin, J.-L. and Le Bras, M., 2002. Alternative Reality: A New Platform for Digital Arts, *ACM Symposium on Virtual Reality Software and Technology* (VRST2003), pp. 100-108, Osaka, Japan, October 2003
7. Forbus, K.D., Qualitative Process Theory, *Artificial Intelligence*, 24, 1-3, pp. 85-168, 1984.
8. Cavazza, M., Hartley, S., Lugrin J.-L. and Le Bras, M., Qualitative Physics in Virtual Environments, ACM Intelligent User Interfaces, pp. 54-61, 2004.
9. Michotte, A., The perception of causality. New York:Basic Books. Translated from the French by T. R. and E.Miles, 1963.
10. Fikes, R. E. and Nilsson, N. J., STRIPS: a new approach to the, application of theorem proving to problem solving. Artificial Intelligence, 2 (3-4), pp. 189-208, 1971.
11. Bec, L., Elements d'Epistemologie Fabulatoire, in: C. Langton, C. Taylor, J.D. Farmer, & S. Rasmussen (Eds.), *Artificial Life II, SFI Studies in the Sciences of Complexity*, Proc. Vol. X. Redwood City, CA: Addison-Wesley, 1991.

Tangible Image Query

Krešimir Matković[1], Thomas Psik[2], Ina Wagner[2], and Werner Purgathofer[3]

[1] VRVis Research Center in Vienna, Austria,
http://www.vrvis.at, Matkovic@VRVis.at
[2] Institute for Design and Assessment of Technology,
Vienna University of Technology, Austria,
http://www.media.tuwien.ac.at, {psik, iwagner}@pop.tuwien.ac.at.at
[3] Institute of Computer Graphics and Algorithms,
Vienna University of Technology, Austria,
http://www.cg.tuwien.ac.at, wp@cg.tuwien.ac.at

Abstract. This paper introduces a tangible user interface for browsing and retrieving images from an image database. The basis for the query to the image database is a color layout sketch, which is used by the underlying query algorithm to find the best matches. The users are provided with colored cubes of various sizes and colors. The users can place and arrange the colored cubes on a small table to create a color layout sketch. Multiple users can use this interface to collaborate in an image query. To evaluate the benefits of the interface, it is compared to a traditional GUI application in which the users use a mouse to paint a color layout sketch. The tangible interface appears to be easier to use and better accepted by people who belive they are unable to draw or paint or who do not want to use computer.

1   Introduction

The explosion of digital technology in the last decade led to an enormous amount of digital images. Conventional ways of data retrieval became just insufficient for large amounts of visual material. Popular thumbnail views are useless, if we have thousands or tens of thousands of images. Another approach, key wording, simple does not work for most of us. It is easy to keyword a few images, but it is illusory to expect that average users will keyword their whole collection of images. Eakins and Graham [1] claim that some professional agencies need up to 40 minutes to keyword a single image. It is clear that common users confronted with hundreds and thousands of images cannot do such precise key wording. Content based image retrieval, which has been a subject of extensive research in the last decade, tries to offer a solution for retrieving images from large databases.

The original and still often used idea is the query by example method. This means that the user supplies an image, and the system tries to find similar images. In this case the central problem is the definition of similarity. As humans themselves can not always agree on what is similar and what is not (or what is more similar) the results of image retrieval are often unexpected and sometimes

A. Butz et al. (Eds.): SG 2004, LNCS 3031, pp. 31–42, 2004.
© Springer-Verlag Berlin Heidelberg 2004

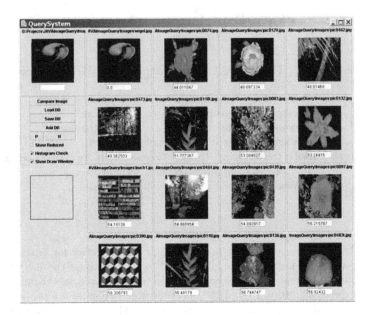

Fig. 1. Query by Example can be disappointing if the user does not understand the underlying algorithm. Here the system searches for a similar color-layout, and not for birds.

disappointing. Figure 1 shows an example where such a system was used to search for images similar to the bird image. If the user understands that the system tries to find images with similar color layout, and not content (bird in this case), results are much more satisfactory. On the other hand if the user expects birds she/he might be really disappointed.

The next step in image retrieval was not to search only for overall similarity, but rather to find images containing a specific pattern. A company logo is a good example. Imagine a company searching for images containing their logo. The logo can be anywhere in the image, it can be taken under various lighting conditions, it can be distorted due to the perspective projection and so on. Clearly this is not a trivial task. Furthermore, if one tries to find all images containing a bird, for example, the whole search becomes practically impossible.

There are numerous systems capable of various kinds of image queries available. IBM's QBIC System [2] was one of the first systems, and it can be tested online at [3, 4]. The VIR Image engine [5] from Virage, Inc. and the Photobook Project [6] developed in the MIT Media Lab are two also well known examples. The work of Jacobs at al. [7] is especially well known in the computer graphics community. All of these as well as [8, 9, 10], represent the query by example approach. There are systems like Blobworld [11, 12] or ICONA [13, 14] which represent another group of systems, they go beyond simple query by example, and try to find similar shapes, textures, and other features.

Some systems offer a possibility for the user to sketch the query image. The basic idea is that a user might remember how the image looked like (but cannot remember the image's name), so the user sketches the image, and the system finds matching images from the database. Another possible scenario of use comes from the designers' and architects' perspective. In the concept design phase of a project it is common practice to browse through image collections in order to be inspired, to see some unexpected connection between images. Visual image query can be used for such a browsing. The drawback of the method described above (see Figure 1) suddenly becomes an advantage. Asking for a parrot, and getting a flower can be either: frustrating or inspiring, depending on the user and the context.

This work is based on such a system, and a new kind of user interface for sketching images is introduced. Instead of using a mouse to draw, users are provided with small cubes of various sizes and colors, and they try to sketch an image using the color cubes. Cubes are placed on a semitransparent glass surface. Besides the cubes, users may use any colored objects. This kind of "sketching" using currently available artifacts is particularly common among designers and architects. We implemented the method, built a prototype and tested it with users. Finally we compared the results with conventional sketching using a mouse.

2   Underlying Algorithm

Although the underlying system is arbitrary, and the method can be combined with any query by example method, we needed one method for our implementation. The system is based on the visual image query by Matkovic et al. [15]. The underlying algorithm will be briefly described. Just like most of the image query methods, the method uses descriptors calculated for each image. These descriptors are created in the database during a preprocessing phase. When the user performs a query, a descriptor is created for the query image and compared to the stored descriptors. Various query systems differ in the way how descriptors (sometimes called signatures) are created. The Visual Image Query (the system he have used) calculates descriptors using 1000 quasi-randomly distributed rectangles of various sizes in the image. The rectangles partly overlap. The sizes of the rectangle are chosen according to the contrast sensitivity function of the human eye. Figure 2 illustrates the distribution at the first 100, 250, 500, and 1000 rectangles. For each rectangle the average color is computed, and all 1000 Luv color triples are stored in the signature. The signature contains only color information for each rectangle, and the system can not distinguish if, e.g., an orange spot in the middle is a flower or a fish. The only information known is that there is an orange spot in the middle. The exact shape of the spot is also not known. It is sampled using the rectangles, and can never be precisely reconstructed. The comparison of two descriptors is done in the Luv color space, i.e. for all 1000 triples the luv-difference is computed and a weighted sum, according to the contrast sensitivity function, of these differences is taken as distance function of the two images.

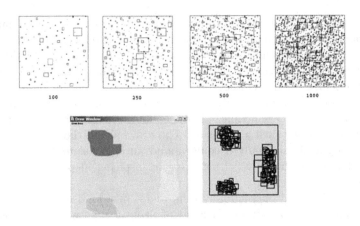

Fig. 2. Top: Rectangle distribution for the first 100, 250, 500 and 1000 rectangles in the algorithm we have used.Bottom: The user draws three separate areas, and only the corresponding rectangles are used for this query.

This method was selected since it is particularly convenient for the comparison of user sketches. The sketch is not precise, and actually, only the color layout matters. However, in order to make it suitable for the new interface, and in order to compare it with conventional input, the original algorithm had to be changed slightly.

2.1   Changes to the Original Algorithm

In the original algorithm the descriptor consists of 1000 Luv triples. Comparing two descriptors means computing the Luv difference for 1000 triples. In order to speed up the process, the algorithm was modified slightly. 1000 rectangles are placed in the image, and the average color of each rectangle is computed. This average color is then rounded to the 64 color set. Now, the descriptor consists of 1000 indexes (in the 64 color set) instead of 1000 Luv triples. The difference between two descriptors can be computed faster using a matrix of predefined differences between all 64 available colors.

In the original algorithm either the whole image or one selected area was compared. This had to be changed to allow multiple areas. Only these parts of the image where the user sketched something will be used in the comparison. In this way the user does not need to sketch the background, but only significant places she/he remembers. Furthermore, the query starts automatically when the user does not change the sketch for a second, and results are displayed. Figure 2 illustrates an example of a simple sketch and the subset of rectangles used in this case. Of course, the support for the new interface had to be added as well.

2.2   Sketching the Query Image

Tests with the original system using conventional mouse input, showed that there are two groups of users. The first group of users, forming a majority, are the users who claim they cannot draw (or paint, or sketch). It was not easy to encourage them to try the system. They were just saying "I can not draw". Although we explained that they do not need to draw an exact reproduction, but just a red spot here, and a blue spot there... just a color layout sketch, it was still not easy to get sketches from them.

The second group of users were users who can draw. The problem with them was that they were not satisfied with the sketch, they wanted to have it perfect.

Some systems are offering tools for drawing circles, rectangles, and other primitives. If such a system is used for color layout search results are even more disappointing. Imagine a user drawing a yellow circle, and the system responding with flower images, or even yellow triangles. Of course, the system was not recognizing the shape, but only the color. This is misleading for the users in most cases.

It was clear that conventional sketching is a good solution only for a very limited number of users. Another kind of interface is needed, an interface that is very suitable for sketching, but which is not suitable for drawing. In this way, users who cannot draw will not be disappointed with their drawing results. It is impossible to draw with that interface anyhow, and for the same reason the users who can draw will not try to draw perfectly. Such an interface is introduced in this paper, and this is the main contribution.

3   New Sketching Interface

The whole setup consists of a table with a semi-transparent white glass plate. There is a set of color cubes, and the users can arrange them on the table in order to make a sketch. A simple web cam is mounted under the plate, which is used to retrieve the color layout sketch. This sketch image is then used as a query image. Figure 3 shows a part of the setup with the table used for sketching. It was common practice during our experiments that users "draw" together. They stood around the table, and instead of the others instructing one user what to do (which was common with the mouse), the group could draw together. The collaboration is another important quality of the cubes interface. Furthermore, not only the cubes can be used to sketch. As soon as a bowl of fruits was placed next to the table, some users used oranges and apples as sketch tools.

4   Vision Based Color Sketch

The Crayon project [16] provides a good overview of the current state of vision based interaction. In the project the researchers use a camera for hand tracking and explored the field of color calibration and machine learning. Our approach is

Fig. 3. Students experimenting with the new interface.

related to their work in the respect that we also extract color information from a live video stream.

Various problems that are related to color vision had to be faced. First tests showed that for certain colors (especially cyan and gray) that were desirable, no stable calibration was possible. This is because web cams provide compressed video information and use optical sensors that are optimized to capture images of faces. The main usage of this kind of camera are video meetings, so the red part of the visual spectrum is covered quite well, but blue and contrast are not of high concern.

4.1   Hardware Setup

To reduce the problems that come with computer vision, like changing ambient light and dynamic in- camera adaption, a setup where these external interferences are reduced was created. The camera was mounted underneath a semi transparent surface, on which the colored cubes were placed. Also a light source was installed underneath this surface to ensure proper lighting conditions. The setup was surrounded by a non transparent casing leaving only the surface visible to the users and exposed to the ambient light in the room. It was possible to achieve good results with a static calibration of the color detector with this setup. The output of the query was displayed by using a projector to create a large screen right in front of the image sketching surface.

The need for such a special hardware setup might be considered to be a drawback of the system. Not everyone has the possibility to allow extra space in the office for such an installation. In such a case a simplified system consisting of a web cam pointing down on the desktop (the real desktop), and a set of colorful cubes, game stones, pieces of paper, or similar things can be used to test the system. Of course, the system is more single user oriented in such a reduced setup, but it suffices for test purposes. Furthermore, the use of flatbed scanners for this purpose was briefly exploited with advantages like better color and contrast but also drawbacks like increased response times and reduced interactivity.

4.2   The Steps of the Color Sketch Retrieval

Two approaches were implemented to create our test setups. In the first implementation the color segmentation was applied at the vision part of the system. First an image is grabbed from the web cam, then a color segmentation is performed and finally a color indexed image is sent to the search engine. The color segmentation was implemented using the HSV (hue, saturation, value) color space. For each color (white, yellow, orange, red, green, blue, magenta, black) ranges for the HSV values are specified. Using a simple filter, regions in the grabbed image that have color values within these ranges are copied to a color index image. The color index range is from 1 to 8. Zero is being used to indicate that none of the colors was detected. This indexed color image is then sent over the network to the search algorithm.

In the second implementation background subtraction was used to filter out the parts of the video stream that have been changed or added by the users. This approach sends a full color image (with reduced size) and an alpha channel (specifying the regions that are not background) to the search engine.

A "change" parameter is extracted from the live stream as well, measuring how much the image has changed between two updates. A high value indicates that the users are currently changing the sketch or just moving the hands within the observed area (for example to point out certain regions and compare them with the results). During this period of vivid interaction no update is sent to the search algorithm, not even the color segmentation or background subtraction is evaluated. Such intermediate results would confuse the users and also distract their concentration from the task of creating or changing a sketch. When the "change" parameter drops below a certain value the image segmentation is activated. If the difference between the resulting sketch and the previous query to the search algorithm is above a certain value (indicating that the vivid change in the video stream was not just moving the hand but also moving some objects), the new sketch is sent to the search algorithm. This makes it possible to create fast update rates, as no unnecessary video images and queries are evaluated.

Both image segmentation approaches have their advantages. The color segmentation provides better results in respect of removing the background and not used areas. Because the background subtraction algorithm dynamically updates the reference image it is more stable to ambient light changes. Also the background subtraction allows the use of more than 8 colors, because the colors are not mapped to one of the indexed colors of the cubes. At the same time the network traffic increases as more data has to be sent to the search engine.

Selection of Colors for the Tangible Interface The original implementation using the mouse as an interface allowed the users to create a sketch with about 50 different colors. Users memorizes only main colors mostly based on the hue value. They tend to use only a basic set of colors when they try to reproduce an image. Therefore to help the users to focus on a basic color sketch, only basic colors where provided in form of colored cubes for the tangible interface. White and black as representatives for the grey spectrum and red, green, blue as the basic colors. As yellow, orange and magenta are also well memorized colors those were provided, too. Early tests with a web cam showed that cyan as a mixture of green and blue is badly captured by web cams. Therefore no cyan cubes were provided for the tests. Feedback from the users proved that cyan is not an important color.

5   Comparing Mouse and Tangible Interface

As discussed in [17] a user interface can be evaluated with the terms: degree of indirection, degree of integration, degree of compatibility. Although the original publication focuses on widgets, it can also be adopted for tangible user interfaces. The object that the interface operates on can be interpreted in two ways. On the one hand the users manipulate the color layout sketch, on the other hand they do that because they want to change the results of the color layout query.

The degree of indirection is a measure of the spatial and temporal offsets generated by an interface. The spatial offset is the distance between the input part of the interface and the object it operates on. The temporal offset is the time difference between the physical action on the interface and the response of the object. The temporal offset is quite the same for both interfaces, as the sketching of the color layout is performed in real time with both interfaces, without any time delay. And after a specific time without manipulation both interfaces send the created sketch to the search algorithm. The spatial offset is slightly better with the mouse interface as the drawing area and the display of the results are on the same screen and the tangible interface needs two separate areas, one to sketch the color layout and one to present the results.

The degree of compatibility measures the similarity between the physical actions of the users on the interface and the response of the object. The tangible user interface provides a higher degree of compatibility as the users directly manipulate the color layout sketch with the colored cubes. The interface is a very direct approach without abstract mapping between input and effect on the query. With the mouse interface the users have to draw by selecting a color from the palette and then move the mouse to create a colored area in the sketching window.

The degree of integration measures the ratio between the degrees of freedom (DOF) provided by the logical part of the instrument and the DOFs captured by the input device. The term degree of integration was introduced in integral tasks [18]. The degree of freedom can be evaluated in two dimensions: the color dimension and the layout (2D) dimension. The mouse interface provides only a 2D interface. Therefore an indirect color selection method has to be incorporated. The tangible interface in our current setup allows direct access to all three dimensions (color and 2D), but as one of our test users stated, the cubes can also be stacked to create a three dimensional structure. So the tangible interface has four dimensions that can be operated on. These do not match with the needed three dimensions, but can be resolved if colored objects are used that cannot be stacked, like half-spheres instead of cubes.

6   Results

We have tested the system with a large number of users. The application was presented at various workshops, including a "Beginner's day" at the university and a workshop that was part of the review of the ATELIER project. Some of the workshops were publicly accessible, therefore different types of users tested the system. The users had different drawing and computer usage skills. The general feedback from the testers was very positive. The tangible interface is very attractive and easy to use.

In addition he have interviewed selected special users, that work with pictures in their profession. A collection of approximately one thousand images was presented to the users. They observed a slideshow, and they were asked to remember a few images that had an impact on them. Afterwards they tried to draw a sketch in order to retrieve the memorized images. First they made a sketch with the mouse, and then using the new color cube interface. Results and impressions of users were compared at the end.

Fig. 4. Sketch done by a painter looking for the portrait of the sitting person.

Figure 4 shows a sketch of a sitting person, and result images (she was looking for the second best guess by the system). Most of the users tried to "draw" the picture with the mouse, and the tangible interface helped them to understand that a sketch is better for the search than a "redraw" of the image they searched for. The results that were presented by the search algorithm often did not fit their expectations when drawing with the mouse (and trying to draw structures). The color they found were missing were mostly brown and grey, but this could correlate with the picture selection. Investigating the multi user aspect of the tangible user interface was also interesting, as some of the users complained about it, when other destroyed their work by changing the sketch without asking.

The general response was very good, and most of the users liked the tangible interface better than conventional one. As we had some test users with visual arts background, we noted that they were very pleased with the surprising component of the tool. E.g., a user searched for a sun-set that was instantly within the top 15, but mixed with images of red flowers and a firework. These results were far from disappointing, and the flowers and firework images fitted well in the users expectations.

7   Conclusion

As many available examples prove the color layout search is an interesting approach to image query. Our work presents a new tangible user interface that allows creating color layout sketches in an easy and straight forward manner. Rather than improving the query algorithm itself, we tried to find a new interface which suits the existing algorithms better. The algorithm needs a certain level of abstraction, which is often hard to achieve using a traditional mouse-interface. The new color cube interface makes it impossible to draw precisely, and therefore helps the users achieve the needed level of abstraction.

Still many of the problems of the underlying methods persist. Tangible user interfaces enrich the possibility of collaboration and multi user input, with all the problems that come with it. For example there is no method of helping the users with synchronization, as all users that use the interface, actually shared this interface physically. They have to sort out conflicts between them without (computational) help, for example: someone adding his ideas to the sketch without asking. The method of color layout image retrieval also has its flaws. Most of the users cannot clearly identify the distinction between shape and color layout. A good example is the search for a sunset. A red shape placed in the middle of the image is a good approach, but images where the sun is not close to the center will not be found, even if it is a picture of a sunset, and images of a red flower in the center of the image will be found instead.

We observed that the use of a tangible user interface helps the users to create color layouts rather than shapes. More over the interface can be used in a more vivid way. It allows direct access to the sketch rather than the indirect method of using a mouse.

The color cubes interface fits very well with the underlying visual image query, and helps the users to cope with the limitations of the query algorithm. In this way the usability of the whole system is significantly enhanced.

8   Future Work

We want to integrate this interface into a framework, where designers are adding images to a repository. These pictures are indexed (with words) and therefore we will be able to do a filtering based on these keywords, also. This will lead to an image query system that combines the unsharp search based on color layout, as described in this article, and image search by keyword. In combining these two approaches we hope to encourage the users of the framework to make use of this interface even more. We want to test whether the combination of indexing by words and a color based image search will result in a better interface or not. The surprise element of results will surely decrease (in case the indexing is done properly), but also the results could fit better to the expectations of the users.

Improvements on the color layout search engine will also be investigated. As we will have access to a repository with over 10.000 images, we can than test the scalability of the algorithm and probably introduce new aspects in respect of clustering the database and improving the response to the query.

The vision system as described in this paper was realized using a consumer web cam. If a high quality camera can be used, surely the detection of the color sketch would improve as the color dynamic will increase.

9   Acknowledgments

The authors would like to thank our co-researchers from the Atelier Project, in particular Andreas Rumpfhuber. This work was partly sponsored by the Atelier project - EU IST-2001-33064. Parts of this work were carried out at the VRVis Research Center in Vienna (`http://www.VRVis.at/`), Austria, which is funded by an Austrian governmental research program called K plus.

References

[1] Eakins, J.P., Graham, M.E.: Content-based image retrieval, a report to the jisc technology applications programme 1999. (Technical report)

[2] Petkovic, D., Niblack, W., Flickner, M., Steele, D., Lee, D., Yin, J., Hafner, J., Tung, F., Treat, H., Dow, R., Gee, M., Vo, M., Vo, P., Holt, B., Hethorn, J., Weiss, K., Elliott, P., Bird, C.: Recent applications of ibm's query by image content (qbic). In: Proceedings of the 1996 ACM symposium on Applied Computing, ACM Press (1996) 2–6

[3] IRS: (Image Retrieval Service (IRS) of the EVlib, http://visinfo.zib.de/irs)

[4] QBIC: (The State Hermitage Museum, St. Petersburg, Russia, QBIC Color and Layout Search, http://www.hermitagemuseum.org/fcgi-bin/db2www/ qbicsearch.mac/qbic?sellang=english)

[5] Gupta, A.: The virage image search engine: an open framework for image management. In: Storage and Retrieval for Image and Video Databases IV, SPIE proceedings series. Volume 2670. (1996) 76–87

[6] Pentland, A., Picard, R., Sclaroff, S.: Photobook: Content-based manipulation of image databases. In: SPIE Storage and Retrieval for Image and Video Databases II, number 2185, Feb. 1994, San Jose, CA. (1994)

[7] Jacobs, C.E., Finkelstein, A., Salesin, D.H.: Fast multiresolution image querying. In: Proceedings of the 22nd annual conference on Computer graphics and interactive techniques, ACM Press (1995) 277–286

[8] Faloutsos, C., Barber, R., Flickner, M., Hafner, J., Niblack, W., Petkovic, D., Equitz, W.: Efficient and effective querying by image content. Journal of Intelligent Information Systems 3 (1994) 231–262

[9] Kelly, P.M., Cannon, M.: Query by image example: The candid approach, los alamos national laboratory white paper (1995)

[10] Vailaya, A., Zhong, Y., Jain, A.: A hierarchical system for efficient image retrieval,. In: Procedeengs of International Conference on Pattern Recognition (August 1996). (1996)

[11] Belongie, S., Carson, C., Greenspan, H., Malik, J.: Color- and texture-based image segmentation using EM and its application to content-based image retrieval. In: Proceedings of the Sixth International Conference on Computer Vision. (1998)

[12] Carson, C., Thomas, M., Belongie, S., Hellerstein, J.M., Malik, J.: Blobworld: A system for region-based image indexing and retrieval. In: Third International Conference on Visual Information Systems, Springer (1999)

[13] Boujemaa, N., Fauqueur, J., Ferecatu, M., Fleuret, F., Gouet, V., Saux, B.L., Sahbi, H.: Ikona for interactive specific and generic image retrieval. In: Proceedings of International workshop on Multimedia Content-Based Indexing and Retrieval (MMCBIR'2001), Rocquencourt, France. (2001)

[14] Fauqueur, J., Boujemaa, N.: Logical query composition from local visual feature thesaurus. In: Proceedings of Third International Workshop on Content-Based Multimedia Indexing (CBMI'03). (2003)

[15] Matkovic, K., Neumann, L., Siglaer, J., Kompast, M., Purgathofer, W.: Visual image query. In: Proceedings of Smart Graphics 2002. (2002)

[16] Fails, J.A., Olsen, D.R.: A design tool for camera-based interaction. In: Proceedings of the ACM CHI 2003 Conference on Human Factors in Computing Systems, Association for Computer Machinery (2003) 449–456

[17] Beaudouin-Lafon, M.: Instrumental interaction: An interaction model for designing post- wimp user interfaces. In: Proceedings of the ACM CHI 2000 Conference on Human Factors in Computing Systems, Association for Computer Machinery (2000) 446–453

[18] Jacob, I., Oliver, J.: Evaluation of techniques for specifying 3d rotations with a 2d input device. In: Proceedings of HCI'95 Conference, People and Computers X. (1995) 63–76

Implementation of ActiveCube as an Intuitive 3D Computer Interface

Ryoichi Watanabe[1], Yuichi Itoh[1], Michihiro Kawai[2],
Yoshifumi Kitamura[1], Fumio Kishino[1], and Hideo Kikuchi[3]

[1] Graduate School of Information Science and Technology, Osaka University
2–1, Yamadaoka, Suita, Osaka, 565–0871, Japan
{ryoichi, itoh, kitamura, kishino}@ist.osaka-u.ac.jp
http://www-human.ist.osaka-u.ac.jp/ActiveCube/
[2] Graduate School of Engineering, Osaka University
Currently with NTT DoCoMo Kansai, Inc.
[3] System Watt Co., Ltd.
4-1-38–4F, Isobedori, Chuo-ku, Kobe, 651-0084, Japan
kikuchi@watt.co.jp

Abstract. This paper describes in details the implementation of the ActiveCube system. ActiveCube allows users to construct and interact with 3D environments by using physical cubes as bi-directional interfaces. A computer recognizes the 3D structure of the connected cubes in real time by utilizing a real-time communication network among the cubes. ActiveCube is also equipped with both input and output devices that are integrated in the cubes and help in making the interaction intuitive and clear. Spatial, temporal and functional consistency is always maintained between the physical object and its corresponding virtual representation. Experimental results demonstrate ActiveCube's potential in achieving natural and intuitive interaction.

1 Introduction

GUIs that use metaphors from the real world have helped to improve the efficiency of various tasks carried out on computers. Recently, a lot of research has been focusing on more flexible and sophisticated user interfaces that use intuition and kansei (sensitivity)-based GUI design. For example, virtual reality research has been utilizing spatial proprioception and experience in 3D environments, and multimodal interfaces have been effectively employing various sensory channels. However, these approaches toward sophisticated user interfaces have suffered from problems: users can still face difficulties in operating or manipulating objects when these do not have proper physical manifestation. Moreover, users are often unsure of the causal relationships between the input device they are using and its expected output. Such uncertainties can result from lack of interface affordance or from spatial separation between the interface action and perception spaces [1].

The approach of direct manipulation can make a user interface easy to learn, to use, and to retain over time [2]. It requires rapid, incremental, and reversible

A. Butz et al. (Eds.): SG 2004, LNCS 3031, pp. 43–53, 2004.
© Springer-Verlag Berlin Heidelberg 2004

actions that can be performed physically. Recently, 3D object shape modeling and interaction has become an essential area of study in computer science. Although there is a lot of literature and proposals for sophisticated interfaces for 3D object shape modeling and interaction based on the approach of direct manipulation, it is still difficult to know where to start if ordinary interaction devices are used because of the complexity of 3D space.

Recent research efforts attempted to design user interfaces that use physically meaningful objects to improve the intuitiveness of 3D object modeling or interactive manipulation. If users were able to construct 3D objects by simply combining physical blocks, the user interface for 3D object shape modeling would become intuitive. Moreover, if the constructed object were to have a functionality to accept the user's input and to express the simulated output results, the user could directly interact with the 3D environment by using the constructed object instead of using ordinary interation devices such as the mouse, keyboard and display monitor. Consequently, the user interface would become more intuitive, and it would be easier to understand what is happening in the virtual environment, because the constructed object would act as a physical replica of the virtual structure.

To achieve these features, we proposed and implemented a user interface called ActiveCube [3]. In this paper we present in details our novel system design and implementation approach. The ActiveCube system allows users to construct and interact with 3D environments using physical cubes with a bi-directional user interface. The computer recognizes the 3D structure of these connected cubes in real time, so consistency is always maintained between the physical object and its corresponding representation in the computer. ActiveCube is equipped with input and output devices, located conveniently on the cubes, which help make the interface intuitive and maintain a clear relationship between the input of the user's operational intention and the output of the simulated results. In this paper, we describe in details the implementation of the ActiveCube system, which achieves real-time 3D modeling, real-time interaction, and a bi-directional user interface. We also present experiments that measure the performance of the ActiveCube system and demonstrate that ActiveCube technology can potentially support natural and intuitive interaction.

2   Related Work

3D object shape modeling by assembling physical blocks is a solution that solves the problem of complexity in 3D space by offering an easy way to recognize a spatial configuration in a 3D environment. Research on 3D object shape modeling using physical blocks to achieve an intuitive interface was carried out in the early days with architecture designs [4] using machine-readable models [5,6]. These ideas were later followed by further efforts [7,8]. Recently, a modeling system was proposed in which the geometry of fully assembled Lego-type blocks is recognized by a computer after a user connects them to the computer and powers the computer on [9]. However, the recognition of the geometry of connected objects in this approach is an offline process and does not work in real-time while a user is connecting or disconnecting blocks. Therefore, one of the most necessary features of direct manipulation [2] is not satisfied in this modeling system.

There is an interaction system designed to run a predetermined program by connecting triangular plains [10], where the object shape can be changed and the geometry of the connected triangular plains can be recognized in real time. However, this system has no input and output devices to interact with. AlgoBlock is based on a similar idea and has a program-coding interface using blocks [11]. In this modeling system using blocks [4,5,6,7,8,9], each block is neither equipped with an input device to obtain the user's operational intention nor an output device to show the simulated results. Therefore, the user never interacts with the 3D environment directly using the constructed blocks.

3   Implementation of ActiveCube

ActiveCube is a set of rigid cubes with 5-cm length edges. Users can construct various 3D structures by combining the cubes as they desire. The faces of the cubes are the same so each cube can be connected to any other cube. A computer recognizes the 3D structure of the connected cubes in real time; therefore, the users can construct a 3D structure in the computer (i.e., in the virtual environment) that exactly corresponds to the physical structure of the physical cubes in the real environment at the current time. ActiveCube is equipped with sensors that obtain the user's operational intention and other information from the real environment. ActiveCube is also equipped with a display system and actuators to show the simulated results or internal status of the computer system. The consistency between the physical 3D structure made from the cubes in the real environment and its representation in the virtual environment is always maintained by utilizing real-time communication channels.

In this section, the implementation details of ActiveCube are described by explaining the hardware and software of the system.

3.1   Hardware

To achieve the functionality of real-time interaction, a real-time network management system called LON (Local Operating Network) technology (Echelon Corporation) is used. In the ActiveCube system, each cube corresponds to a small-scale intelligence unit called a node, and an exclusive chip called the Neuron Chip (Toshiba Corporation TTMPN3120FE3M) is used to control each node. This chip is incorporated into ActiveCube. The Neuron Chip consists of three 8-bit processors: one for controlling and executing application programs and two for network communications. It is equipped with RAM of 2 Kbytes, ROM of 16 Kbytes, EEPROM of 2 Kbytes, two timer counter channels, and can run at 20 MHz. The chip achieves a speed of 39 Kbps for communications with other chips.

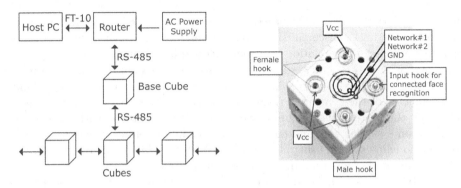

Fig. 1. ActiveCube system configuration.

Fig. 2. Arrangement of contact terminals.

An ID number is assigned to each cube (cube ID) for the unique identification of cubes. An ID number is also assigned to each face (face ID) of the cube to identify the connecting faces. The connected cubes constitute a network where a parallel RS-485 port enables communications between cubes. The cubes are connected to the host PC through a special cube called the base cube as shown in Figure 1. Communications is achieved between the cubes and host PC by translating RS-485 to FT-10 on a router. Four electro communication lines are needed on each face for communications between the cubes. For this purpose, four contact terminals are arranged on each face: communication #1, communication #2, Vcc, and GND as shown in Figure 2. Here, three of four hooks for physical connection of adjacent cubes are used to supply power (Vcc), and one of them is allocated as an input hook in order to recognize the connection of the other cube onto this face.

3.2 Software

The executable programs for each cube, coded in NeuronC, are compiled and written in the non-volatile memory on each Neuron Chip. These programs comprise two parts. The first part detects the connected face, and the other controls the input or output device. The software installed on the host PC is coded in Visual Basic and uses the ActiveCube library based on ActiveX technology. By using this library, all cubes and the host PC can communicate directly with each other. At the same time, the host PC can receive simultaneous input data from all of the input cubes and control each output cube directly.

4 Real-Time 3D Modeling

A method of real-time recognition of a 3D structure constructed with connected cubes to support real-time 3D modeling is described here.

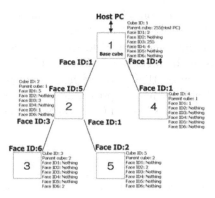

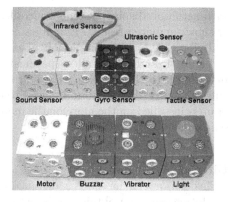

Fig. 3. Example of connection-status tree(CS-tree).

Fig. 4. Examples of ActiveCube with input/output

When a user connects or disconnects a cube, each cube can recognize faces that are connected or disconnected by receiving the face recognition signal changes from the faces of the other cubes. Because the host PC can monitor the face recognition signals of all faces of each cube in real time, it works to update the status of the connections of the cubes from this information. A connection-status tree (CS-tree) is used to manage the connection status information, by storing cube IDs and connected face IDs in its nodes (see Figure 3). The constant updating of the CS-tree enables the real-time recognition of all connections/disconnections. Therefore, the important point is to recognize the faces that are connected or disconnected.

When a new cube (a child cube) is connected to a cube that has already been connected to the network (a parent cube), the child cube is supplied with power, which allows it to broadcast its cube ID and connected face ID. Here, the connected face ID is determined by detecting the Vcc supplied to the input hook for connected face recognition from the connected cube. At the same time, the parent cube broadcasts its cube ID and connected face ID. By using this information, the host PC updates the CS-tree and recognizes the 3D structure. If the cube is later disconnected, the parent cube broadcasts its face ID indicating that the input signal (Vcc) is extinct, and the host PC cuts the nodes of the disconnected cubes and updates the CS-tree.

5 Bi-directional User Interface and Real-Time Interaction

5.1 Input/Output Devices of ActiveCube

Because each cube is equipped with a Neuron Chip, it is possible to control the sensors to obtain the user's operational intention and other environmental information. The sensors can be ultrasonic, gyroscopic, tactile, infrared, luminous, and temperature sensors. It is also possible for a cube to be equipped with actuator/display systems controlled by a Neuron Chip to execute actions or show simulated results. Examples of such devices are lights, buzzers, motors, and vibrators. Some examples of cubes with input and output devices are shown in Figure 4, and the detailed specifications of these cubes are described below. In addition to the following, there are plain cubes that have neither input nor output devices. Plain cubes are used to enrich the shape representation. A program is installed on the non-volatile memory of each Neuron Chip to control the sensing devices or actuators.

Ultrasonic Sensor

This sensor can measure a distance of between 4 cm to 29 cm with 0.1cm resolution, and can obtain the intention of the user by measuring the distance from the palm or other objects. The other specifications of the sensor include a 16mm diameter, 55-degree directivity, and 40 kHz frequency.

Gyroscopic Sensor

This sensor measures 3D orientations. It can measure the relative rotational angles around the X, Y, and Z coordinate axes with 256 resolution based on the initial orientation when the cube is connected.

Tactile Sensor

A cube can be equipped with up to two tactile sensors; each can detect eight directional touches. They enable operations such as the control of virtual objects or the degree of mouse click.

Infrared Sensor

This sensor is capable of light-emission division with infrared rays (950 nm) and reception (780-1000 nm) and can distinguish whether an object exists near the sensor (within an approximately 20-mm distance).

Light

Light can be independently emitted in the three primary colors of red, green, and blue with one LED, with 256 levels. The LED has three different modes, i.e., fast blinking, slow blinking, and constant. It can be used to show simulation results.

Buzzer

The buzzer can emit not only a single tone but also various musical scales. It has nine different modes such as an intermittent sound, continuous sound, siren, and so on. It can also be used to indicate simulation results.

Motor

The speed, direction, and amount of rotation of the motor can be controlled. The rotating shaft of the motor extends externally from the cube, so it can be equipped with propellers, tires, etc. The major specifications of the motor include a 1800 pulse/rotation encoder resolution, 255:1 gear ratio, 44gcm torque, 4W, and 4-60 rpm.

Vibrator

The on/off and frequency of the vibrator can be controlled.

5.2 Implementation of Applications

The application on the host PC determines the operation of the entire Active-Cube system. As we have described, by using the ActiveCube library, an application can analyze a 3D structure, show the simulation results on the display, and transmit operational commands to the cubes connected to the network. The causal relationships between the input devices and the output devices can also be determined by the application on the host PC. For example, the brightness of the light can vary with the distance measured by the ultrasonic sensor, and the color of the light can vary with the measured orientation by the gyroscopic sensor. The distance measured by the ultrasonic sensor can also change the rotational speed of the motor, frequency of the vibrator, and so on. Here, combinations among multiple input and multiple output devices can be considered simultaneously.

Each cube has a unique function, and an object that has various purposes as a whole can be constructed by assembling multiple cubes. The function of each cube can be flexibly changed with the connected positions/orientations or the assembled object shape.

6 Experiments

In this section, the performance of the ActiveCube system is measured through experiments, in order to make sure that the system satisfies the requirements to support natural and intuitive interactions.

6.1 Experiment Method

In the experiments, we use four kinds of cubes, i.e., light cubes, plain cubes, a base cube, and a ping cube. The ping cube is programmed to reply to a message from the host PC immediately, upon receiving a message from the host PC. Three experiments are conducted as follows.

Experiment 1: Communication Time between the Host PC and Cubes

The communication time between the host PC and cubes is measured. The message from the host PC reaches the ping cube via the base cube and some plain cubes. After receiving this message, the ping cube sends a message to the host PC via the same cubes. The time is measured by the timer in the software on the host PC (PentiumIII 600MHz, 192MB, XGA 13.3 inch). Here, the distance is defined by the number of plain cubes between the base cube and the ping cube, i.e., if there is no plain cube, the distance is determined as one; or, if there is one plain cube, the distance is determined as two. In this experiment, we measure the distance from one to six, i.e., from zero to five plain cubes, and we try five hundred times at each distance.

Experiment 2: Operation Completion Time from Command Transmission from the Host PC to the Output Cube

We measure the time from the command transmission by the host PC, ordering a light cube to turn on its light, to the actual light-up of the cube. At first, a base cube and a light cube are connected to the network. Next, when a certain button on the display of the host PC is pressed, the host PC sends a command to the light cube to turn on its light. At the same time, the color of the label on the display of the host PC is changed. Identical to experiment 1, some plain cubes are connected between the base cube and light cube. The distance is changed from one to three, and we carry out measurements ten times from the change of the color of the label to the light-up of the cube. As the measurement apparatus, we use a digital video camera (NTSC, 29.97fps=33.4msec/frame).

Experiment 3: Recognition Time of Connection and Disconnection

The recognition time of connection and disconnection using both methods is measured. Concretely, we connect and disconnect the light cube to/from the base cube, and then measure the time when the host PC recognizes the connection/disconnection. At first, the light cube, which is programmed to turn on its light upon receiving supplied power, is used. When the light cube is connected to the base cube, the light is turned on. Then, if the host PC recognizes this connection, the color of the label on the display of the host PC is changed. Similarly, when the light cube is disconnected, the light is turned off, and then, if the host PC recognizes this disconnection, the color of the label on the display of the host PC is changed. We measure the time that the host PC recognizes the connection and disconnection ten times by using a digital video camera.

6.2   Results

Figure 5 shows the result of experiment 1. As can be recognized, the communication time between the host PC and cubes is almost the same even if the number of cubes is increased, and the total average is 248.2 msec. When the host PC receives data from an input cube, it performs polling to the input cube. Therefore, this result can be considered as the response time to the input data from the input cubes. From the result of experiment 2 (see Figure 6), we find that the average time from the command transmission by the host PC to complete the operation of the output device of the cube is 447.6 msec. The operation completion time from the command transmission is almost the same even if the number of cubes is increased. The reason why both graphs of Figure 5 and 6 are almost flat with the numbers of cubes is that the network structure used in the ActiveCube system is parallel. From the result of experiment 3, the average recognition time of the connection of the cube is 1282.6 msec (standard deviation is 82.1 msec), and that of the disconnection of the cube is 898.5 msec (standard deviation is 29.2 msec).

6.3   Discussion

Generally, the response time of a user interface is considered to be appropriate to the task, e.g., in simple frequent tasks, the user will feel comfortable with the user interface if the response time is around 1 second [12]. From all of the results measured by experiments 1, 2, and 3, the response time of interaction (inputting the user's intention with input cubes, getting the simulated results with output cubes, and constructing a 3D structure by connecting or disconnecting cubes) with ActiveCube is less than about 1 second and this result shows that the system has a sufficient performance to support natural and intuitive interactions.

In actual applications using the ActiveCube system, we can usually expect the processes measured in experiments 1, 2, and 3 to be executed all together. However, we cannot usually expect the user to connect or disconnect cubes and interact with the devices at the same time. Moreover, we can regard the response time as the sum of the results of the time values measured in experiments 1 and 2, when the user receives output data from the output device of the cube as a result of his/her input to the input device of the cube. Therefore, the average response time will be 695.8 msec, which is considered to be sufficient for the user to interact naturally and intuitively. However, because the process that controls the output cubes and inputs data from the input cubes is not parallel but serial, the response time to complete all operations will take a long time if the number of cubes that should be controlled is increased. However, during this process, because at least one of the input/output devices of the connected cubes will be activated, the no-response time will be less than 1 second.

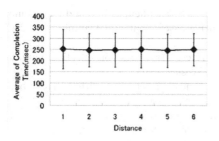
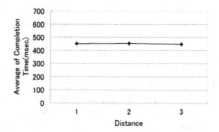
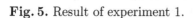

Fig. 5. Result of experiment 1.   **Fig. 6.** Result of experiment 2.

With Lego-type blocks [9], the computation time for shape recognition increases with the number of connected cubes. For example, it has been reported that 35 seconds are required to recognize 98 connected cubes and 53 minutes for 560 cubes. On the other hand, in ActiveCube, the time for recognition does not increase even if the number of cubes is increased as shown in Figures 5 and 6. Here, almost 150 cubes can be connected when the distance value in experiment 1 is 6. This difference comes from the fact that the network structure of ActiveCube is parallel, while that of the Logo-type blocks is serial.

7 Summary

We proposed the ActiveCube system to allow users to construct and interact with 3D environments using cubes with bi-directional user interface. A computer recognizes the constructed 3D structure in real time, and maintains consistency between the physical object and its corresponding representation on the computer in terms of object shape and functionality. Furthermore, the user can construct and interact with the 3D environment using the cubes in real time and intuitively. We conducted experiments to measure the performance of the ActiveCube system. The experimental results showed that ActiveCube can potentially support natural and intuitive interaction.

As future work, we are planning to improve the ActiveCube system by implementing various sensors and displays/actuators, and by developing applications that will fully exploit the functions of ActiveCube.

8 Acknowledgement

This research was supported in part by "The 21st Century Center of Excellence Program" of the Ministry of Education, Culture, Sports, Science and Technology, Japan and by Exploratory Software Project grant of Information-technology Promotion Agency, Japan.

References

1. E. Sharlin, Y. Itoh, B.A. Watson, Y. Kitamura, S. Sutphen, L. Liu, and F. Kishino, "Spatial tangible user interfaces for cognitive assessment and training," Proc of Bio-ADIT 2004, pp.410–425, 2004.
2. B. Shneiderman, Designing the user interface: strategies for effective human-computer interaction, 3rd edition, Addison-Wesley, 1998.
3. Y. Kitamura, Y. Itoh and F. Kishino, "Real-time 3D interaction with ActiveCube," CHI 2001 Extended Abstracts, pp.355–356, 2001.
4. R. Aish and P. Noakes, "Architecture without numbers - CAAD based on a 3D modeling system," Computer-Aided Design, vol.16, No.6, pp.321–328, 1984.
5. J.H. Frazer, An evolutionary architecture, Architectural Association, 1995.
6. J.H. Frazer, J.M. Frazer, and P.A. Frazer, "Three-dimensional data input devices," Proc. of Conference on Computers/Graphics in the Building Process, 1982.

7. G. Anagnostou, D. Dewey, and A.T. Patera, "Geometry-defining processors for engineering design and analysis," The Visual Computer, 5, pp.304–315, 1989.
8. M. Resnick, F. Martin, R. Sargent, and B. Silverman, "Programmable bricks: toys to think with," IBM Systems Journal, vol.35, No.3–4, pp.443–452, 1996.
9. D. Anderson, J. Frankel, J. Marks, A. Agarwala, P. Beardsley, J. Hodgins, D. Leigh, K. Ryall, E. Sullivan and J.S. Yedidia, "Tangible interaction + graphical interpretation: a new approach to 3D modeling," Proc. of SIGGRAPH 2000, pp.393–402, 2000.
10. M.G. Gorbet, M. Orth, and H. Ishii, "Triangles: tangible interface for manipulation and exploration of digital information topography," Conference on Human Factors in Computing Systems (Proc. of ACM CHI '98), pp.49–56, 1998.
11. H. Suzuki and H. Kato, "AlgoBlock: a tangible programming language, a tool for collaborative learning," Proc. of 4th European Logo Conference, pp.297–303, 1993.
12. T.W. Butler, "Computer response time and user performance," Conference on Human Factors in Computing Systems (Proc. of ACM CHI '83), pp.56–62. 1983.

Stage-Based Augmented Edutainment

Rainer Malaka*, Kerstin Schneider*, Ursula Kretschmer**

*European Media Laboratory, Heidelberg
[firstname.lastname]@eml-d.villa-bosch.de
** University of Freiburg, Institute for Forest Growth

Abstract. Augmented Reality (AR) in the real world is still an unsolved task. Beyond toy systems there are no scalable solutions for outdoor systems that include augmented real-time graphics. The problems are multifold: rendering capacities, tracking problems, data handling and gaps in coverage of tracking and/or graphic data. Our approach introduces an edutainment system that presents an AR system for edutainment. We work around these problems through a stage-based approach for AR. Stages are AR-islands in the real world, where selected functions can be performed. The stages are connected through a navigational system that links them together. For our application domain, an edutainment system, we employ a digital story telling scenario that links the stages semantically. Human computer-interaction in the proposed system is through a multi-modal interface that can be accessed through various devices. The advantage of our stage-based system is scalability and robustness of an outdoor and real-world AR system.

Introduction

Today's AR systems for pedestrians are not yet ready for widespread use. They are still mostly artifacts in research labs. AR becomes quite successful in limited application domains where users are bound to some specialized activity. For instance in medicine, AR systems can help to augment the doctor's reality for finding a tumor during a medical treatment [4]. The advantage for the system design is that the user is known, the environment is static and many effects such as illumination or unknown environmental factors can be neglected. This makes tracking easy and stable systems can be built. For pedestrian systems that aim at augmenting city parts such as buildings or routes, a number of problems occur that make tracking and augmented display much more complex than in well-defined static systems. First of all, the complexity increases due to the mere size of the outdoor world. In contrast to a room or a building, a city or even a part of a city such as the old town of Heidelberg, Germany, is larger and more complex than indoor AR settings. Many simple techniques for tracking that can be used indoors are not possible any more either because of their growing costs or because of proprietary reasons. For instance AR-tags can easily be put in a factory hall or on lab walls and be used for tracking, but it is too expensive to put them onto every wall of every house in a city. Moreover, the owner of the buildings might not allow that or people might find it very ugly if historical sights like a medieval castle are spotted with these tags. Even more, weather

A. Butz et al. (Eds.): SG 2004, LNCS 3031, pp. 54-65, 2004.
© Springer-Verlag Berlin Heidelberg 2004

conditions, birds or other influences may soon make the tags unreadable and they would have to be refreshed quite often. There is no real alternative to video-based tracking for AR systems in a city for pedestrians. But this is also extremely difficult and its complexity is much higher than in indoor scenarios. Weather conditions may lead to varying illuminations every moment. Cloudy days not only may change temporally but also spatially the illumination scene of a video image. There are seasonal variations like snow in winter, lost leaves in fall and green trees in summer that can change scenery in one square dramatically during a year. And of course, video-based tracking is not only difficult, but also expensive. The system needs a rich basis of sampled images, textures, polygons to be matched with the recorded image and the computational effort for the matching is very hard to be done in real-time when the AR system has to do 25 renderings per second. Due to these facts, most actual systems are not scalable and cover only a small area of an outdoor location. They can hardly be scaled up to a system that can guide a user through a city. Therefore smart graphics solutions are needed to work around these problems and to allow for "some" AR in city environments.

In our system, we took these problems into account and propose a stage-based system that models AR-scenes at different stages that are located in the city. Only on these predefined stages, AR and video-tracking is possible. To link these stages, a user is guided through the city and between the stages by a navigational system, where a story engine presents a story that links the different stages together. In the first realization of such a stage-based AR-system, we implemented an edutainment system where children are led through a city and where the stages represent historical important sites. Each stage is limited in space and therefore, tracking and rendering can be done efficiently for each stage. The story that is moderated and presented by virtual characters leads the user from one stage to the other. Thus, the user's impression is not that there is only sparse AR information, but that there is a pervasive system with AR islands that belong together. This approach allows for easy scalability, because new stages can be easily defined and integrated. The story acts as a binding glue both spatially and semantically. Additionally, the users should have the possibility to ask for extensive, detailed, and auxiliary information regarding buildings, events, persons, living conditions, etc., related to the spatial buildings or the story to satisfy their interest aroused. In the following, we present the stage-based edutainment system in more detail.

The goal of our system is to explain to students a history lesson about the 30 Years' War, a European period in the 17th century [6]. As location for the system we chose the city of Heidelberg, a German city that has been captured in this war by foreign troupes. Goal of the AR components is to give an on-sight impression of the historical situation. The students walk independently around Heidelberg in search of 'ghosts'. This is the reason why our project is called GEIST[1]. They carry a mobile PC and a portable display. On the predefined stages the story takes place. Figure 1 shows a map of Heidelberg indicating places where the story can take place. For these stages 3D reconstructions of ancient buildings need to be modeled and precise information about historical facts and fictional data are gathered.

---

[1] The term 'Geist' means 'ghost' in English.

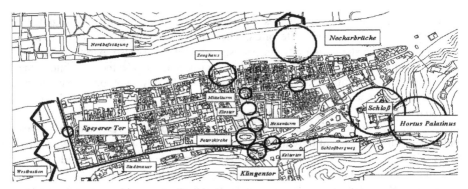

Figure 1: Historical sites with 3D reconstructions where the story can take place

When the users enter one of these sites, they hear a ghost-like sound. This indicates to them that they should use their displays. They look through it and are then able to watch 3D reconstructions of the buildings. They feel as if they are in a historical scene. In front of these buildings ghosts appear and tell the students episodes about their own life 400 years ago. This is realized by combining historical and fictional details about the 30 Years' War in Heidelberg.

Knowledge Base

Comprehensive and detailed, geographical and historical information is captured in a knowledge base. It is based on four interconnected (heterogeneous) databases, each storing and managing data within a specific scope. A query engine breaks down complex questions into particular database queries and then reassembles the particular answers of the databases into proper results. Figure 2 shows an overview of the databases and system components.

The first database, a GIS (Geographic Information System), is used in combination with a smart tracking system. The spatial information can be used to navigate the user or to show them on a map where an interesting place is. The database also contains information about the geography of Heidelberg during the 30 Years' War. This enables us to relate historical facts to current spatial locations or regions.

The Architecture Base (AB) is the basis for all graphical rendering of historical buildings and stores 3D reconstructions of the ancient buildings [6]. These reconstructions are then the scenery on which the ghosts will tell their stories. To position the ghosts closely and accurately we store models of whole buildings as well as models of building parts forming an aggregation (i.e., part-of) hierarchy. The problem of modeling ancient buildings, which are not there any more, is that the person who is doing the modeling needs to interpret old engravings or plans in the right way. Furthermore this information is by no means complete, so the modelers' knowledge and even imagination has to come into play. Research of similar buildings in remote cities can be used for getting a clue about the kind of material and colors of the ancient building. All this information is linked to the reconstruction data. This helps detect changes in interpretation as soon as new information is gathered.

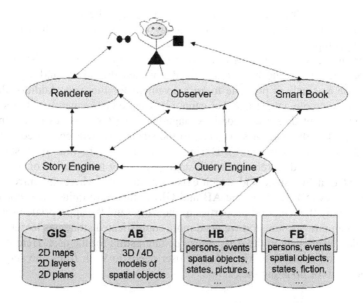

Figure 2: Databases and system components in the GEIST system

Different models of the same area or object representing several levels of detail or knowledge can be stored at the same time.

All historical facts are stored in the History Base (HB) (e.g., information about historical events, actors, living conditions, professions, spatial objects, and the usage of historical buildings). A system for querying this type of data must be able to handle imprecision and fuzziness (e.g., a historical event happened during or around a certain time point; this is not exactly defined). We need to be able to model, store and compare information that contains fuzzy descriptions of time, location and even contents (religious, political, etc.). Additionally it is necessary to model the manifold interrelationships of the historical information pieces. For example, to understand history it is necessary to have knowledge about the interrelationships between historical processes and/or states. These relationships are important for describing complex and nested historical actions and they allow us to model causes and effects of processes and states represented as information pieces in our database. We developed an ontology for history that will help us model historical facts (events, processes, states, actors, roles, spatial objects, functions, etc.), in such a way that we can then perform complex queries based on this model and even reason about the relation between the different facts. The information pieces are classified according to different user classes (e.g., pupils, students, experts).

Fictional information is stored in the Fiction Base (FB). Fictional elements are obtained from a combination of legends, non-proofed historical information, theories and related historical facts. The AB contains, aside from the historical models, also 3D models of buildings or other spatial objects that are fictional. The information corresponding to these models is then stored in the FB and not in the HB.

To answer queries concerning the current location of the user, e.g. if the user is located in a story-relevant place (i.e., a stage) or queries related to the current scene of the story or to the general contents of the story, the query engine will require information from other components, namely the Story Engine, the Observer and the tracking component.

One of the main problems to address is that on the one hand the amount of data will be huge, requiring big storage needs, and on the other hand a portable system should be as small as possible to be convenient for the user. Additionally, wireless access to a remote database server cannot be ensured permanently. Thus strategies for caching relevant data are needed. A stage-based system enables us to single out the data related to the current story (i.e., to the stages that will be visited in the story or only those in the near future). During the users' sojourn time on a stage he needs mainly access to data related to this stage (e.g., only information of buildings which are located at this stage and which existed at the time where the current story takes place is relevant). Caching the AB and GIS is therefore quite easy. For caching the HB data only the temporal properties of the story (and the appropriate user class) need to be taken into account and we need more sophisticated strategies to determine which of its data is relevant to the story or can be interesting for the user. Here it is important not to be too restrictive. The time the user needs to walk from one stage to another can be used for updating the cache.

Augmented Reality

Several AR systems for application areas in an outdoor environment have been developed. There are systems only based on the results of sensors [5,10]. They lack of accuracy and show problems due to narrow streets in case of GPS (Global Positioning System) or when walking close to magnetic disturbances by using a gyro tracker. The latter can be taken into account with a map of these disturbances [1]. To enable better results video-based techniques have been implemented in a new generation of outdoor AR systems. They can help to control the prediction and the errors of the orientation sensor [16]. But they are also used to connect the view of the person to the real environment. This is done by use of a reference. This is either a digital elevation model [2], or a 3D GIS [3], a photo [14], or prepared parts of photo-realistic building models [12]. The systems are either complex in preparation of the data or not yet feasible for real-time applications [15]. They all work only in specially prepared environments. That means they are not complete solutions for use in a whole city. In our tracking system we combine a very accurate AR system on particular places, namely stages for the ghosts of our story, with the coverage of localization in the total area. To do so, we use several sensors and tracking techniques. Besides GPS and an orientation tracker, a video-based approach has been developed. It determines accurate position and orientation in an urban environment. The basis is a comparison between the video stream of a camera, which the user carries with the mobile display and a 3D model of the surroundings. The position sensor and the orientation tracker give a good restriction of the data, which should be used out of the 3D data for comparison. After finding correspondent features in the camera image and in the 3D model, the relative orientation between the real position and the captured results of the sensors can be determined. The outcomes are a translation vector and a rotation matrix between the real and a virtual camera, which was used to get data out of the

3D model. By use of these results the position and line of sight of the user can be determined. Figure 3 shows an overview of the video tracking approach.

As this kind of determining the position and orientation is very time intensive, we use a frame-to-frame comparison to enable real-time computation for a longer time period. Once, position and orientation are calculated by use of the 3D model, the relative orientation between the camera position of one frame and the position of the next is sufficient. As soon as there is an evaluation possible, which shows that the results are no longer sufficient, or after a short time period the high accurate 3D model based tracking technique is again applied to the system.

The position and orientation results are managed by a component, which uses a prediction and filtering technique. If there are several information units from different sensors or techniques available the results can be merged or particular outcome can be left out. This is the reason, why each sensor or technique is described by parameters. Together with the current evaluation, which is calculated after each prediction, the combination of the sensor results can be determined after matching it to the requirements of the system, of the users and of the environment.

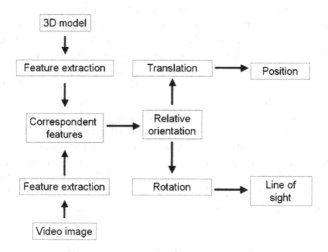

Figure 3: Video tracking based on a 3D model

The AR system contains a knowledge base, which stores information about the user and about the environment. It also reacts to current information, which is observed during runtime. The component is called Observer (Figure 2).

While following the story, the most important influence of the tracking requirements is the position, which effects the combination of the sensors. The following example is illustrated in Figure 4. All the time, position information of the players is captured. Using the GPS device can do this, as long as the streets are not too narrow or too many trees block or disturb the satellite signal. An alternative is the use of a mobile cellular network. As soon as new navigation information is gathered, it is matched with the GIS. Here, the exact location of the stages is stored. As soon as the person enters one of these stages, the GIS registers this information. The combination of a GPS sensor and an orientation tracker is not sufficient for the fading in of reconstructions in the visual field of a person. The video tracking approach is applied to the system. Alternative information, which is gathered by sensors are weather changes, which can lead to a faster finish of the story. Time pressure while using navigational guidance forces the user to know or guess most of the facts and the system only assists him by finding his way through the city.

Mediation of History through an Active Story

The information content and in particular the AR reconstructions of ancient buildings is embedded into a story [8]. A story engine that incorporates the stage-based approach for AR used in the system drives this story (Figure 2). In order to edit stories, an authoring environment has been built. An author can provide historical information about the 30 Years' War of Heidelberg and provide further multimedia information concerning interesting places/stages or persons being part of the GEIST story. The basis for the GEIST story builds a story model based on the Propp model for fairy tales. Vladimir Propp, a Russian formalist, has investigated a lot of research work in the analysis of fairy tales and extracted significant functions and components being part in all of these stories [11]. Typical examples for these functions are an introduction, an arising problem, and the appearance of a hero or the problem solution supported by the hero. Hence, users/authors build an individual story based on the framework of the Propp story model and describe various scenes of the GEIST story. They decide, which ghosts represented by virtual characters appear at which place and which information is provided at the different places [13]. One stage in our current setting is, for instance a gallery in the Castle Garden (Figure 5). Here, the user can view the reconstructed columns and between these columns, a ghost can appear and tell the user about his history. With regard to interaction and communication between users such as pupils as a special visitor group of Heidelberg different interaction metaphors are defined [9]. Further on, pedagogical elements such as didactic methods and concepts are integrated within the final GEIST story in order to generate a fruitful

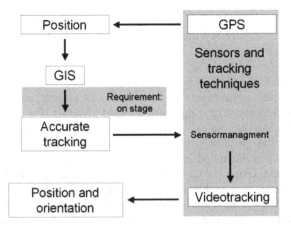

Figure 4: Influence of requirements on the selection of sensors or tracking techniques

Figure 5: One of the stages at the Heidelberg Castle. Left: original picture with wire-frame reconstructions of the destroyed columns. Right: AR view with reconstructed column gallery.

learning environment. The story is exported as XML file of the authoring tool and loaded into the Story Engine during run-time of the GEIST system.

The Story Engine gets information from the Observer as soon as the person enters one of the stages. On these places accurate information is transmitted to this component. Among this information is data indicating which buildings the users looks at. The Story Engine determines which reconstruction should be faded in, where ghosts should appear and what they tell the user. The story not only consists of the propagation of fictional elements and historical facts but also of questions or instructions to the user who is actively involved into the story line. S/he determines which way the story takes. Depending on the user's decisions or answers the story turns a specific way. Every user experiences his/her own story. It depends also on the way the users walk, which stages they enter in which order, how long they stay on one of the stages. All of this information is gathered and stored within the Observer and offered to the story during the whole runtime process. At the end, all users will have experienced a tensing story with a happy ending.

If users look for more information, they can use the Smart Book (i.e., a history information system) with a user interface on a PDA (Personal Digital Assistant). As shown in Figure 2, it is the direct access to the knowledge base. Here, they can watch 3D reconstructions, learn about the sovereigns of that epoch or delve into the life of everyday people of the past. The user should have the possibility to ask for extensive, detailed, and auxiliary information regarding buildings, events, persons, living conditions, etc., related to the story that he or she is submerged into.

Beside answering questions like "Show me a map of Heidelberg around the year 1618 highlighting the spatial objects for which information is available" or "Who was the elector Palatine in 1633?" it is necessary to show timelines of historical processes, causation graphs or other graphical representation which are useful for highlighting the multifarious relationships of events or states during the 30 Years' War. The presented scope, time period and granularity should be user definable.

Figure 6: n'vision's portable display with the Intertrax 2

The stage-oriented interface that we develop helps the user to find information in an easy and fast manner.

First Prototype

At this moment, the system covers independent stages where the story takes place and where ghosts appear. The position of the user is tracked wherever during his walk the GPS signal is available. We employ a Trimble DGPS receiver based on the correction signal of the German satellite positioning service. Every change in position is notified to the GIS. As soon as a person enters one of the stages a part of the story is built up and the scene is presented to the user. This requires additional information about the head orientation. The system automatically switches on Intersense's Intertrax 2, a gyroscopic headtracker. Then, reconstructions on the accurate position are presented in the portable display and ghosts appear in front of them to tell their story. The combination of different tracking sensors is implemented by use of a Kalman filter methodology. To allow new sensors to be integrated into the project the programmed connections need to comply to specific interfaces. As soon as the videotracking component is completed it will also be attached. Until then, only DGPS and the orientation tracker are applied to the system. With our DGPS device we get position results up to 40 cm. The reliability of the orientation tracker is sufficient to show short scenes which give the user an AR impression where ghost-like avatars appear in front of historic reconstructions. To allow a more stable system, the videotracking component will be the AR solution for an urban environment. For the visual presentation of the rendered scenes, we are using n'vision's VB 30 display. Figure 6 shows the hardware for information presentation in our AR system.

The user influences the content of the story by determining the order of the stages. But also decisions as reactions of answers or invitations of the ghosts effect the story. In the current version not only input by use of a finger mouse is possible but also help by a magic map is feasible. The user can take the map out of the pocket if he needs information about his current position. The system notices this and sends this information to the Story Engine. The current scene is stopped as soon as possible and the user is invited to watch the map. The current position is indicated as a symbol in the wearable display and the position of that symbol aligns exactly with the user's position in the map.

The Smart Book allows searching; querying, browsing, and navigation through the content of the history base (see Figure 7). The user has a lot of possibilities to define search conditions. For example, when searching an event s/he can define certain actors who were involved, the region where the event has happened, and time conditions, etc.

For the better understanding of history it is necessary to present the information in a way that the multifarious interrelationships between the information pieces are visible intelligibly to the user. The smart book dynamically retrieves, composes and rearranges relevant sets of interesting information pieces to point out important coherences in history or to put them into perspective.

To handle the manifold fuzzy, imprecise and incomplete temporal information in an efficient manner, we use new object-oriented features of object-relational database systems by integrating a hierarchy of temporal user-defined types together with many user-defined type functions (according to our ontology of time). Additionally, we worked on a temporal extension of XPath [5] to be able to store and manage fuzzy temporal information in XML format or XML databases as well.

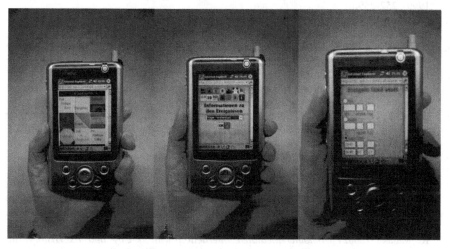

Figure 7: The Smart Book (in German)

Conclusions

We presented our outdoor AR system, which is included in a story and offered to the user as an interactive story. While interacting with and searching for ghosts to get information about the 30 Years' War in Heidelberg the users experience the ancient environment and learn how people used to live 400 years ago. Digital story telling, Augmented Reality and intelligent access to several data bases are merged building a system to offer information about the current location wherever the users are interested or where parts of the story take place. A large area of the city is covered by the system but only on predefined places accurate tracking of position and orientation is required which makes smart AR visualizations feasible. While using the merging of different tracking techniques in one system we enable real-time localization results depending on the information the user can get access to.

Acknowledgements

The authors would like to thank all co-workers in the GEIST project at EML, FhG-IGD, and ZGDV for their contributions and fruitful discussions. Parts of this work was funded by the German Ministry for Education and Research (BMBF) and by the Klaus Tschira Foundation.

References

1. R. Azuma, B. Hoff, H. Neely III, and R. Sarfaty. A Motion-Stabilized Outdoor Augmented Reality System. Proceedings of IEEE VR '99 (Houston, TX, 13-17 March 1999), 252-259.
2. R. Behringer. Registration for Outdoor Augmented Reality Applications Using Computer Vision Techniques and Hybrid Sensors. Proceedings of IEEE VR '99, 244-251.
3. T. Chen and R. Shibasaki. A Versatile AR Type 3D MobileGIS Based on Image Navigation Technology. IEEE 1999, 1070-1075
4. Falk V, Gummert, Walther, Hayase, Berry, Mohr (1999): Quality of Computer Enhanced Totally Endoscopic Coronary Bypass Graft Anastomosis Comparison to Conventional Technique. Eur J Cardiothorac Surg 1999; 13:260-266
5. S. Feiner, B. MacIntyre, T. Höllerer., and A. Webster. A Touring Machine: Prototyping 3D Mobile Augmented Reality Systems for Exploring the Urban Environment. IEEE 1997, 74-81
6. Kalb, M., Schneider, K., Specht, G.: TXpath: ein temporales Modell für XML-Datenbanken, BTW, Leipzig, 2003.
7. Kretschmer, U., Coors, V., Spierling, U., Grasbon, D., Schneider, K., Rojas, I., Malaka, R.: Meeting the Spirit of History. In Proceedings of the International Symposium on Virtual Reality, Archaeology and Cultural Heritage, VAST 2001, Glyfada, Nr Athens, Greece, 28-30 November 2001.
8. R. Malaka (2002) *Computer-Mediated Interaction with a City and Its History.* In: Workshop notes of the International Workshop on Intelligent Media Technology for Communicative Reality, held at PRICAI 2002, Tokyo, pp. 24-29.
9. Mateas, M.; Stern, A. (2000): Towards integrating plot and character for interactive drama. K. Dautenhahn, editor, Proccedings of the 2000 Fall Symposium: Socially Intelligent Agents: The Human in the Loop, pages 113 – 118. AAAI Press, Menlo Park, CA.
10. W. Piekarski, B. Gunther, and B. Thomas. Integrating Virtual and Augmented Realities in an Outdoor Application. Proceedings of International Workshop on Augmented Reality1999, 45-54
11. Propp V. (1958): Morphology of the folktale. International Journal of American Linguistics, 24(4)
12. M. Ribo, P. Lang, H. Ganster., M. Brandner, C. Stock, and A. Pinz. Hybrid Tracking for Outdoor Augmented Reality Applications. IEEE Computer Graphics and Applications, November/December 2002 issue, 54-63
13. Spierling, U.; Grasbon, D.; Braun, N.; Iurgel, I (2002): Setting the scene: playing digital director in interactive storytelling and creation. Elsevier Computers & Graphics 26, 1, 31-44.

14. D. Stricker. Tracking with Reference Images: A Real-Time and Markerless Tracking Solution for Out-Door Augmented Reality Applications. Proceedings of VAST 2001 – Virtual Reality, Archaeology, and Cultural Heritage. Glyfada, Greece.
15. J. Teichert, R. Malaka (2002) *A Component Association Architecture for Image Understanding*. In: Proceedings of the International Conference on Artificial Neural Networks, ICANN 2002.
16. S. You, U. Neumann, and R. Azuma. OrientationTracking for Outdoor AR Registration. Proceedings of IEEEVirtual Reality 1999, Houston, Texas, USA.

Retrieving Vector Graphics Using Sketches

Manuel J. Fonseca, Bruno Barroso, Pedro Ribeiro, and Joaquim A. Jorge

Department of Information Systems and Computer Science
INESC-ID/IST/Technical University of Lisbon
R. Alves Redol, 9, 1000-029 Lisboa, Portugal
mjf@inesc-id.pt, {bamb,pdsr}@mega.ist.utl.pt, jaj@inesc-id.pt

Abstract. In this paper we present an approach to allow indexing and retrieving vector graphics by content, using topological and geometric information automatically extracted from figures. The method described retrieves WMF ClipArt files as an instance of the general problem of searching vector drawings. Our prototype can already handle databases with thousands of drawings using commodity hardware. Our scheme uses pattern recognition to identify shapes ensuring good precision vs recall trade-offs, when compared to other approaches. Preliminary usability assessments show promising results and suggest good acceptance of sketching as a query mechanism by users.

1 Introduction

Currently there are a lot of drawings available for integration into documents, either on the Internet or on clip art collections sold in optical media. However, when users decide to integrate an existing figure into a document, they have to browse through large and deep file directories or navigate a complex maze of categories previously defined to organize pictures. Furthermore, such search becomes humanly impossible when the number of drawings increases.

We propose an automatic visual classification scheme based on geometry and spatial relationships, which are better suited to this problem. This is because it takes advantage of users' visual memory and explores their ability to sketch as a query mechanism. We use an indexing method that efficiently supports large sets of drawings, in combination with new schemes that allow us to hierarchically describe drawings and subparts of drawings by level of detail. Finally, we implemented graph-based techniques to compute descriptors for such drawings in a form suitable for machine processing.

The rest of this paper is organized as follows: Section 2 provides an overview of related work in content-based retrieval. In section 3 we describe our approach for content-based retrieval of vector drawings. Section 4 explains, with some detail, our simplification heuristics. In section 5 we present experimental results from preliminary tests with users. Finally we discuss our conclusions and present directions for further research.

A. Butz et al. (Eds.): SG 2004, LNCS 3031, pp. 66–76, 2004.
© Springer-Verlag Berlin Heidelberg 2004

2   Related Work

Recently there has been considerable interest in querying Multimedia databases by content. However, most such work has focused on image databases as surveyed by Shi-Kuo Chang [1]. Similarly, in Rui et al.'s survey [16] the authors analyze several image retrieval systems that use color and texture as main features to describe image content. On the other hand, drawings in electronic format are represented in structured form (vector graphics) requiring different approaches from image-based methods, which resort to color and texture as the main features to describe image content.

Gross's Electronic Cocktail Napkin [11] addressed a visual retrieval scheme based on diagrams, to indexing databases of architectural drawings. Users draw sketches of buildings, which are compared with annotations (diagrams), stored in a database and manually produced by users. Even though this system works well for small sets of drawings, the lack of automatic indexation and classification makes it difficult to scale the approach to large collections of drawings.

Park describes an approach [15] to retrieve mechanical parts based on the dominant shape. Objects are described by recursively decomposing its shape into a dominant shape, auxiliary components and their spatial relationships. The small set of geometric primitives and the not-so-efficient matching algorithm make it hard to handle large databases of drawings.

Funkhouser et. al. [10] describe a method for retrieving 3D shapes using sketched countours. However, their approach relies on silhouettes and their fitting to projections of 3D images, unlike our method which is based on structural matching of graphical contituents using both shape and spatial relations.

Leung and Chen proposed a sketch retrieval method [13] for general unstructured free-form hand-drawings stored in the form of multiple strokes. They use shape information from each stroke exploiting the geometric relationship between multiple strokes for matching. More recently, authors improved their system by also considering spatial relationships between strokes [14]. Authors use a graph based description, similar to ours [7], but describing only inclusion, while we also describe adjacency. However, their technique has two drawbacks. First, they use a restricted number of basic shapes (circle, line and polygon) to classify strokes. Second, it is difficult to scale this method to deal with large databases of drawings, since they explicitly compare the query with all the drawings in the database.

Looking at the majority of the existing content-based retrieval systems for vector drawings, we can observe two things. The first is scalability: most published works use databases with few elements (less than 100). The second is complexity: drawings stored in the database are simple elements not representing sets of real drawings, such as technical drawings or ClipArt drawings.

Our approach to retrieve drawings by content uses spatial relationships and geometric information. From these we derive a hierarchical description mechanism to describe drawings and sketched queries. Additionally, fast and efficient algorithms to perform similarity matching between sketched queries and a large database of ClipArt drawings are required, which we will describe in the following sections.

3   Our Approach

Our method solves both scalability and complexity problems by developing a mechanism for retrieving vector drawings, in electronic format through hand-sketched queries, taking advantage of user's natural ability at sketching and drawing. Unlike the majority of systems cited in the previous section, our technique supports indexing large sets of drawings. To that end, we devised a multidimensional indexing structure that scales well with growing data set size.

3.1   Classification

Content-based retrieval of pictorial data, such as digital images, drawings or graphics, uses features extracted from the corresponding picture. Typically, two kinds of features are used. Visual features encode information, such as color, texture and shape. Relationship features describe topological and spatial relationships among objects in a picture. While digital images rely mainly on color and texture to describe their content, for vector drawings these features are irrelevant. Thus, we focus on topology and geometry. Topology plays an important role on the description of drawings, because users always explore the spatial arrangement of query elements to convey more information.

Our classification process starts by applying a simplification step, to eliminate most useless elements. We try to remove visual details (i.e. small-scale features) while retaining the perceptually dominant elements and shapes in a drawing, in order to speed up queries.

After simplification we identify visual elements, namely polygons and lines, and extract shape and topological information from drawings, using two relationships, **Inclusion** and **Adjacency**, which are a simplified subset of the relationships defined by Max Egenhofer [4]. In this work, Egenhofer divides spatial relationships into directional and topological relations. The most frequently used directional relationships are north, south, east, west, northeast, northwest,

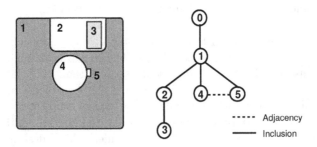

Fig. 1. ClipArt drawing (left) and correspondent topology graph (right).

southeast and southwest. For topological relationships Egenhofer has presented a set of eight distinct relations between two planar regions, namely `disjoint`, `contain`, `inside`, `meet`, `equal`, `cover`, `covered-by` and `overlap`. We group these into three main categories: `Disjoint`, `Adjacent`, which includes `meet` and `overlap`, and `Inclusion`, which spans the other five classes. The relationships thus extracted are then compiled in a Topology Graph, where "parent" edges mean `Inclusion` and "sibling" connections mean `Adjacency`, as illustrated in Figure 1. Even though our relationships are less discriminating than Egenhofer's original set, they hold regardless of rotation and translation. Evidently, the limitations of this scheme lie in that only two very simple spatial relations are considered. While this may not seem very effective for simple, trivial graphics, it becomes more and more efficient as the structure of drawings increases.

However, topology graphs are not directly used for searching similar drawings, since graph matching is a NP-complete problem. We use the corresponding graph spectra instead. For each topology graph to be indexed in a database we compute descriptors based on its spectrum [2]. In this way, we reduce the problem of isomorphism between topology graphs to computing distances between descriptors. To support partial drawing matches, we also compute descriptors for sub-graphs of the main graph. Moreover, we use a new way to describe drawings hierarchically, by dividing them in different levels of detail and then computing descriptors at each level. This combination of sub-graph descriptors and levels of detail, provides a powerful way to describe and search both for drawings or sub-parts of drawings, which is a novel feature of our work. To compute the graph spectrum we start by determining the eigenvalues of its adjacency matrix. The resulting descriptors are multidimensional vectors, whose size depends on graph (and corresponding drawing) complexity. Very complex drawings will yield descriptors with higher dimensions, while simple drawings will result in descriptors with lower size. Figure 2 illustrates how descriptors are computed for the example shown. Descriptors are sorted from highest to lowest value and stored in a database indexing all graphs. It can be shown that descriptors computed in this manner are stable with respect to small changes in graph topology [2]. Furthermore, from experiences performed with 100,000 randomly generated graphs versus a set of 10 candidate similar graphs, we have observed that collisions with descriptors of very different graphs still allow us to retrieve the most likely graphs reliably.

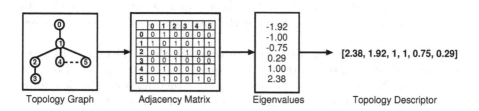

| Topology Graph | Adjacency Matrix | Eigenvalues | Topology Descriptor |

Fig. 2. Topology descriptor computation for drawing of Figure 1.

To acquire geometric information about drawings we use a general shape recognition library which is able to identify a set of geometric shapes and gestural commands called CALI [6, 5]. This enables us to use either drawing data or sketches as input, which is a desirable feature of our system, as we shall see later on. Furthermore it allows us to use geometric features instead of polygon classifications. In this manner we can index and store potentially unlimited families of shapes. We obtain a complete description of geometry in a drawing, by applying this method to each geometric entity of the drawing and as a result we get a multidimensional feature vector that describes its geometry. The geometry and topology descriptors thus computed are inserted in two different indexing structures, one for topological information and another for geometric information, respectively.

3.2   Query

Our system includes a Calligraphic Interface [12] to support the specification of hand-sketched queries, to supplement and overcoming limitations of conventional textual methods. The query component performs the same steps as the classification process, namely simplification, topological and geometric feature extraction, topology graph creation and descriptor computation. This symmetrical approach is unique to our method. In an elegant fashion two types of different information (vector drawings + sketches) are processed by the same pipeline.

We developed a new multidimensional indexing structure, the NB-Tree [8, 9], which provides an efficient indexing mechanism for high–dimensional data points of variable dimension. The NB-Tree is a simple, yet efficient indexing structure for high–dimensional data points of variable dimension, using dimension reduction. It maps multidimensional points to a 1D line by computing their Euclidean Norm. In a second step we sort these points using a B^+-Tree on which we perform all subsequent operations. Moreover, we exploit B^+-Tree efficient sequential search to develop simple, yet performant methods to implement point, range and nearest-neighbor queries.

Computing the similarity between a hand-sketched query and all drawings in a database can entail prohibitive costs especially when we consider large sets of drawings. To speed up searching, we divide our matching scheme in a three-step procedure as shown in Figure 3. The first step searches for topologically similar drawings, working as a first filter to avoid unnecessary geometric matches between false candidates. In the second step we use geometric information to further refine the set of candidates. Finally, we apply a comparison method to get a measure of similarity between the sketched query and drawings retrieved from the database.

Our matching procedure first ranks drawings in the database according to their topological similarity to the sketched query. This is accomplished by performing a KNN query to the topology indexing structure, using the descriptor computed from the sketched query. Results returned by the indexing structure represent a set of descriptors similar (near in the space) to the query descriptor. Each returned descriptor correspond to a specific graph or subgraph stored in

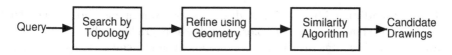

Fig. 3. Block diagram for the matching process.

the topology database, which will be used in the geometry matching. Filtering based on topology drastically reduces the number of drawings to compare, by selecting only drawings with a high likelihood of being similar to the sketched query.

4   Simplification Heuristics

Although the WMF format specify primitives to draw circles, ellipses, rectangles and other regular geometric shapes, most analyzed drawings were only built of polylines, polygons and polypolygons. Taking this into account, we studied the content of several WMF ClipArts to identify particularities that could be used to eliminate useless elements from drawings. The majority of WMF drawings analyzed have lots of information (polygons and lines) only to convey details and visual effects. However, most of this information can be discarded, simplifying drawings without losing meaning.

To simplify drawings we use heuristics that explore their specific features and human perception. This reduces both the information present in drawings, storage space and processing time. Before applying any heuristics, we used the Douglas-Pecker algorithm [3] to reduce the number of points from polygons and lines. This reduction in the number of points greatly speeds up the overall simplification process. We then apply heuristics to reduce figure count in three particularities common to most ClipArt drawings: gradients, contours and small area polygons. Figure 4 illustrates the application of all heuristics. In the following paragraphs we present these simplification heuristics by the order they must be applied.

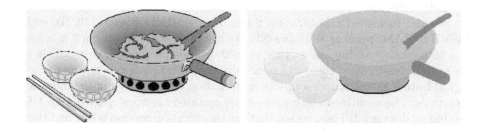

Fig. 4. Application of all heuristics. Original (left) with 281 polygons and simplified (right) with 13 polygons.

Color Gradient: Many ClipArt drawings use continuous and overlapped polygons with small changes in color, to achieve a gradient effect. Since our approach describes drawings using only topology and geometry, color is not relevant for retrieval. However, we use color information to simplify drawings, by grouping polygons with a similar color into a single polygon.

Contour Lines: We found out that many shapes were defined using two polygons, one to specify the filled region and another just to define the contour. Since the second polygon do not convey any additional information, this heuristic goal is to eliminate them.

Small Area Polygons: ClipArt drawings have a lot of small area polygons, which do not convey relevant information. These small polygons usually describe details that users ignore during the specification of a query. This heuristic discards all polygons with an area smaller than a specific value, computed as a percentage of the area of the largest polygon in the drawing. The biggest challenge of this heuristic was the definition of the correct percentage. To that end we simplified drawings using several percentages and asked users to analyze simplified drawings. We also considered trade-offs between simplification and returned results.

5   Evaluation and Experimental Results

As previously discussed, content-based retrieval of drawings comprises two phases. Classification analyzes and converts drawings into logical descriptors. Matching tries to find similar drawings within a set of such descriptors. Whereas the critical step in classification (using our approach) is drawing simplification, in nearest neighbor matching search dominates the resource usage.

To determine the degree of simplification achieved by our heuristics, we randomly selected a sample of 30 drawings and applied the three heuristics described above. We counted the number of polygons and lines before and after applying the heuristics. We found out that on most "typical" WMF drawings extracted from a sample Clipart CD, we can achieve a simplification degree of around 80%, on average, for lines and polygons or above 87%, if we consider line simplification. It is important to notice that after applying these simplification heuristics, users still recognize drawings.

We also measured classification times on a AMD Duron @ 1.3GHz with 448MB of RAM, running Windows XP. We classified 968 drawings in 7 minutes and 55 seconds, yielding an average of 0.49 seconds per each drawing. This is the overall classification time, which includes simplification, geometric and topological feature extraction, descriptors computation and insertion in the indexing structures. The resulting indexing structures required a storage space of 16.8 MB (excluding drawings). Thus, we see that the classification process is fast and that the storage space required is relatively small, making this approach potentially suitable for large data sets of drawings.

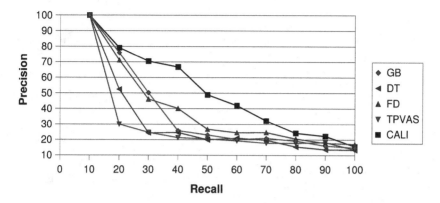

Fig. 5. Recall-Precision comparison.

5.1   Shape Representation

In order to evaluate the retrieval effectiveness (*i.e.* accuracy) of our method, we measured recall and precision figures. Recall is the percentage of similar drawings retrieved with respect to the total number of similar drawings in the database, and precision is the percentage of similar drawings retrieved with respect to the total number of retrieved drawings.

We compared our method to describe shapes (CALI) with four other methods, namely Fourier descriptors (FD), grid-based (GB), Delaunay triangulation (DT) and Touch-point-vertex-angle-sequence (TPVAS). To that end we started from results of an experiment previously performed by Safar [17], where he compared his method (TPVAS) with the FD, GB and DT methods. To that end authors used a database containing 100 contours of fish shapes[1]. From the set of 100 shapes in the database, five were selected randomly as queries. Before measuring the effectiveness of all methods, Safar performed a perception experiment where users had to select (from the database) the ten most similar to each query. So, at the end, they had the ten perceptually most similar results that each query must produce.

We repeated this experiment, using the same database and the same queries, using our method. First we computed descriptors for each of the 100 shapes in the data set and inserted them in our indexing structure (NB-Tree). Then for each query, we computed the correspondent descriptor and used it to perform a nearest-neighbor search in the NB-Tree. Returned results are in decreasing order of similarity to the query. For each of the five queries, we determined the positions for the 10 similar shapes in the ordered response set. Using results from our method and the values presented in Table 2 from [17] we derived the precision-recall plot shown in Figure 5.

---

[1] This database is available from ftp://ftp.ee.surrey.ac.uk/pub/vision/misc/ fish_contours.tar.Z

Fig. 6. ClipArt finder prototype.

Looking at Figure 5 we can see that our technique outperforms all the other methods, yielding good precision figures for recall values up to 50%.

5.2   ClipArt Retrieval

Using the techniques described in this paper, we developed a prototype to retrieve ClipArt drawings, called Bajavista[2]. Our system allows retrieving sets of drawings similar to a hand-sketched query. Figure 6 depicts a screen-shot of our application. On the top-left we can see the sketch of a cloud and on the bottom results returned by the implied query. These results are ordered from left to right, with the most similar on the left. It is also possible to perform Query-by-Example allowing the user to select a result and use it as a the next query, since our classification scheme handles graphics and sketches in the same manner.

In order to assess acceptance and recognition-level performance, we conducted preliminary usability tests involving twelve users. For these tests, we used a database of 968 ClipArt drawings from several categories (food, transportation, etc.). These drawings were classified using our hierarchical scheme to derive descriptors for each level of detail and for each subpart. Resulting descriptors were then inserted into two databases, one for topology and another for geometry, using our NB-Tree.

We gave users a brief description of our prototype, before asking them to perform any of the two planned tasks. We used a Wacom Cintiq LCD digitizing tablet and a cordless stylus to sketch queries.

Task 1 comprises the searching of a drawing by providing them with a verbal description of objects. The main goal of this task was to measure user satisfaction

---

[2] More information can be found in http://immi.inesc.pt/projects/bajavista/

about returned results. We told users they could use Query-by-Example, to get at more results. The outcome from this task revealed that searching by sketch was in general less successful than by Query-by-Example. This is due mainly to the way people drew what was described verbally. Query times, using an AMD Duron @ 1.3GHz were between 1 and 2 seconds, which most users found satisfactory.

In Task 2 we asked users to search for drawings provided by us. The goal of this experiment was to check in what position of the result list the corresponding drawing appeared. Experimental results revealed best performance for drawings with rich topological information or for drawings made of simple geometric shapes. Conversely, drawings with lots of detail or containing hard to draw shapes yielded poor results.

In summary, our system performs better for drawings which contain collections of easy-to-draw shapes, with a strong topological component. In these cases, the topological filtering is effective and reduces the number of drawings to compare in the geometric matching. Furthermore, easy-to-draw shapes assure that users will sketch something very similar to what is stored in the database.

After the experiment we asked users to answer a questionnaire, to obtain feedback about the general functionality of the prototype. Users liked the interaction paradigm very much (sketches as queries), even though some did not like the idea of sketching "too much detail" when looking for more complex drawings. They were satisfied with the returned results and pleased with the short time they had to spend to get what they wanted in contrast to more traditional approaches.

6 Conclusions

We have presented a generic approach suitable for content-based retrieval of structured graphics and drawings. Our method hinges on recasting the general picture matching problem as an instance of graph matching using vector descriptors. To this end we index drawings using a *topology graph* which describes adjacency and containment relations for parts and subparts. We then transform these graphs into descriptor vectors in a way similar to hashing to obviate the need to perform costly graph-isomorphism computations over large databases, using spectral information from graphs. Finally, a novel approach to multidimensional indexing provides the means to efficiently retrieve sub-drawings that match a given query in terms of its topology.

Acknowledgements

This work was funded in part by the Portuguese Foundation for Science and Technology grant 34672/99 and the European Commission project SmartSketches grant# IST-2000-28169. The authors would like to thank Prof. Maytham Safar for providing them with all the information about their human perception experiment.

References

[1] S. K. Chang, B. Perry, and A. Rosenfeld. *Content-Based Multimedia Information Access*. Kluwer Press, 1999.

[2] Dragos Cvetkovic, Peter Rowlinson, and Slobodan Simic. *Eigenspaces of Graphs*. Cambridge University Press, United Kingdom, 1997.

[3] David Douglas and Thomas Peucker. Algorithms for the reduction of the number of points required to represent a digitized line or its caricature. *The Canadian Cartographer*, 10(2):112–122, 1973.

[4] Max J. Egenhofer and Khaled K. Al-Taha. Reasoning about Gradual Changes of Topological Relationships. In A. Frank, I. Campari, and U. Formentini, editors, *Theory and Methods of Spatio-Temporal Reasoning in Geographic Space*, volume 639 of *Lecture Notes in Computer Science*, pages 196–219. Springer-Verlag, Pisa, Italy, September 1992.

[5] Manuel J. Fonseca and Joaquim A. Jorge. CALI : A Software Library for Calligraphic Interfaces. INESC-ID, http://immi.inesc-id.pt/cali/, 2000.

[6] Manuel J. Fonseca and Joaquim A. Jorge. Experimental Evaluation of an on-line Scribble Recognizer. *Pattern Recognition Letters*, 22(12):1311–1319, 2001.

[7] Manuel J. Fonseca and Joaquim A. Jorge. Towards Content-Based Retrieval of Technical Drawings through High-Dimensional Indexing. In *Proceedings of the 1st Ibero-American Symposium in Computer Graphics (SIACG'02)*, pages 263–270, Guimarães, Portugal, July 2002.

[8] Manuel J. Fonseca and Joaquim A. Jorge. Indexing High-Dimensional Data for Content-Based Retrieval in Large Databases. In *Proceedings of the 8th Int. Conference on Database Systems for Advanced Applications (DASFAA'03)*, pages 267–274, Kyoto, Japan, March 2003. IEEE Computer Society Press.

[9] Manuel J. Fonseca and Joaquim A. Jorge. Indexing High-Dimensional Data for Content-Based Retrieval in Large Databases. Technical report, INESC-ID, http://virtual.inesc-id.pt/tr/mjf-jaj-TR-01-03.pdf, 2003.

[10] Thomas Funkhouser, Patrick Min, Michael Kazhdan, Joyce Chen, Alex Halderman, David Dobkin, and David Jacobs. A search engine for 3d models. *ACM Transactions on Graphics*, 22(1), 2003.

[11] Mark Gross and Ellen Do. Demonstrating the Electronic Cocktail Napkin: a paper-like interface for early design. In *Proc. of the Conf. on Human Factors in Computing Systems (CHI'96)*, pages 5–6, 1996.

[12] Joaquim A. Jorge. *Parsing Adjacency Grammars for Calligraphic Interfaces*. PhD thesis, Rensselaer Polytechnic Institute, Troy, New York - USA, December 1994.

[13] Wing Ho Leung and Tsuhan Chen. User-Independent Retrieval of Free-Form Hand-Drawn Sketches. In *Proc. of the IEEE ICASSP'02*, volume 2, pages 2029–2032, Orlando, Florida, USA, May 2002. IEEE Press.

[14] Wing Ho Leung and Tsuhan Chen. Hierarchical Matching for Retrieval of Hand-Drawn Sketches. In *Proc. of the IEEE Int. Conf. on Multimedia and Expo. (ICME'03)*, volume 2, pages 29–32, Baltimore, USA, July 2003. IEEE Press.

[15] Jong Park and Bong Um. A New Approach to Similarity Retrieval of 2D Graphic Objects Based on Dominant Shapes. *Pattern Recog. Letters*, 20:591–616, 1999.

[16] Yong Rui, Thomas S. Huang, and Shih-Fu Chang. Image Retrieval: Current Techniques, Promising Directions, and Open Issues. *Journal of Visual Communication and Image Representation*, 10(1):39–62, March 1999.

[17] Maytham Safar, Cyrus Shahabi, and Chung hao Tan. Resiliency and Robustness of Alternative Shape-Based Image Retrieval Techniques. In *Proc. of IEEE Int. Database Engineering and Applications Symposium*, 2000.

Quality Metrics for 2D Scatterplot Graphics: Automatically Reducing Visual Clutter

Enrico Bertini and Giuseppe Santucci

Università degli Studi di Roma "La Sapienza"
Dipartimento di Informatica e Sistemistica
Via Salaria, 113 - 00198 Roma, Italy
{bertini, santucci}@dis.uniroma1.it

Abstract. The problem of visualizing huge amounts of data is very well known in the field of Computer Graphics. Visualizing large number of items (the order of millions) forces almost any kind of techniques to reveal its limits in terms of expressivity and scalability. To deal with this problem we propose a "feature preservation" approach, based on the idea of modelling the final visualization in a virtual space in order to analyze its features (e.g, absolute and relative density, clusters, etc.). Through this approach we provide a formal model to measure the visual clutter resulting from the representation of a large dataset on a physical device, obtaining some figures about the visualization decay and devising an automatic sampling strategy able to preserve relative densities.

1   Introduction

When visualizing graphics containing large amounts of data a common problem often arises: the image is cluttered. The user suffers from a strong sense of mess that rises by both the intrinsic limits of visual devices and the adopted techniques. Reaching the edge of about one million of items, almost any kind of visual techniques fails to convey detailed information; a lot of graphical elements overlap and many pixels become over plotted, loosing useful pieces of information.

We address this problem following two main paths: first we provide a formal framework to measure the amount of degradation resulting from a given visualization, then we build, upon these measures, an automatic sampling strategy that aims at reducing such a degradation.

Here we analyze a very common situation, in which the visualization is obtained plotting points on a bi-dimensional space, analyzing the loss of information derived by overlapping pixels and screen saturation. We define a formal model that estimates the amount of overlapping elements in a given area and, consequently, the remaining free space. These pieces of information give an objective indication of what is eventually visualized on the physical device; exploiting such measures we can estimate the quality of the displayed graphic devising techniques able to recover the decayed visualization.

A. Butz et al. (Eds.): SG 2004, LNCS 3031, pp. 77–89, 2004.
© Springer-Verlag Berlin Heidelberg 2004

To eliminate the sense of clutter, we employ sampling techniques that, by reducing the number of displayed elements, leave space to more intelligible representations. The challenge is to understand *how much* to sample in order to preserve the visual characteristics of the underlying data. It is quite evident, in fact, that a too strong sampling is useless and destroys the less dense areas, while a too light sampling does not reduce the image cluttering. The formal model we discuss in the paper gives precise indications on the right amount of data sampling in order to produce a representation preserving the most important image characteristics. In this paper we focus on relative density that is one of the main clues the user can grasp from such a kind of graphic and we sample the data in a way that preserves, as much as possible, density differences.

The contribution of this paper is twofold:

1. it presents a novel model that allows for defining and measuring data density both in terms of a virtual space and of a physical space (e.g., a display);
2. it defines a quality metric that allows for (a) estimating the image decay and (b) finding out the right amount of sampling for a certain data set.

The paper is structured as follows: Section 2 analyzes related works, Section 3 describes the model we use to characterize clutter and density, Section 4 deals with the problem of preserving density, formalizing the problem, Section 5 describes some implementation issues, and, finally, Section 6 presents some conclusions and open problems.

2   Related Work

Our research deals with different topics concerning the visualization of data; essentially: metrics for information visualization and techniques to address the problem of visual clutter. In the following we present some related proposals.

2.1   Metrics for Information Visualization

The lack of metrics and evaluation techniques able to give precise indications on how effectively a particular visualization presents data, is still an open problem. As expressed in [9] Information Visualization needs methods to measure the *goodness* of a given visualization. Some preliminary ideas have been proposed that consider both formal measurements and guidelines to follow.

One of the author that first gave indications is E.Tufte, that in his seminal work "The Visual Display of Quantitative Information" [12], proposes some measures to estimate the quality of 2D representations of static data. He proposes measures like: the *data-ink ratio* that represents, *the proportion of a graphic's ink devoted to the non-redundant display of data information* or the *lie factor*, that is the ratio of the size of an effect as shown graphically to its size in the data, or yet, the *data density* that takes into account the size of the graphic in relation to the amount of data displayed. Such measures have been proposed for paper based representations, and are not directly applicable to interactive, computer based visualizations.

Brath in [10] defines new metrics for static 3D images starting from the Tufte's proposal. In particular, he proposes metrics such as the *number of data points* (the number of discrete data values represented on the screen at an instant) and *data density* (number of data points/number of pixels) that resemble the Tufte's approach together with new ones, aiming at measuring the visual image complexity. The *number of simultaneous dimensions displayed* aims at giving an estimation of complexity measuring the number of data attributes that are displayed at the same time. The *occlusion percentage*, provide a measure of occluded elements in the visual space suggesting to reduce such value as much as possible. The *number of identifiable points*, is the number of visible data points identifiable in relationship with every other visible data point. These metrics are interesting and are more appropriate for describing digital representations. However, as stated by the author, they are still immature and need refinements.

While the metrics described here aim at measuring a general goodness or at comparing different visual systems, our aim is to measure the accuracy of the visualization, that is, how well it represents the characteristics hidden inside data. They present some similarities with past metrics but operate at a lower level dealing with pixels and data points, providing measures that can directly be exploited to drive corrective actions. We will describe a model to measure and predict the amount of overlapping pixels and remaining free space. Then we will propose a metric that permits to calculate how well the the relative densities are represented in the current display for scatter-plots. It is worth to note that, on the contrary of the above proposals, we will show how the suggested metrics can be exploited *in practice* to take quantitative decisions about corrective actions and enhance the current visualization.

2.2   Dealing with Visual Density and Clutter

The problem of eliminating visual clutter to produce clearer graphics has been considered in many techniques employed in information visualization systems. Some of them requires some form of interaction (see, e.g.,[1], [2], [4] [8]) others, closer to our approach, use some form of algorithms to produce a non-cluttered image. Among them, *Clustering* is a very common technique (e.g., [11][5]) that originates form data mining field. The idea is to aggregate elements that, according to a measure of similarity, are close together. Visual density is reduced substituting all the elements that are inside a cluster with only one representative graphical element. The drawback is that the data is represented at a higher level of abstraction therefore detail is lost. *Space-filling techniques* permit to construct visualization without overlapping elements by dividing the visual space in sub-areas so that each element has its own place. In [7] space filling curves are followed to assign a single pixel to each element of a database. In [6] the space is split recursively to represent hierarchical data. *Constant density displays* [13][14] consist in giving more details in less dense areas and less details in denser areas permitting the screen space to be optimally utilized. The problem with this approach is that the overall trend of data is generally lost and some distortions are introduced. *Sampling* is used in [3] to reduce the density of visual representation. The idea is to use the sampling tools provided by commercial DBMS, to collect from the database only a sample of the entire dataset. As the authors state, if the sampling is made in random way the distribution is preserved and though it is still possible to grasp some useful information about data correlation and distributions, permitting *"to see the overall trends in the visualization but at a reduced density"*. Even if very interesting, this idea is not free of drawbacks. In particular, when the data present particular distributions, i.e., the data set has both very high and very low density areas, choosing the right amount of sampling is a challenging task. Depending on the amount of sampling two problems can arise:

- If the sampling is too *strong* the areas in which the density is under a certain level become completely empty;
- If the sampling is too *weak* the areas with highest densities will still look all the same (i.e., completely saturated) and consequently the density differences among them will be not perceived by the user.

Our approach differs from the above proposals for three main aspects:

- it provides a sound model for defining in both a virtual and physical space several metrics intended specifically for digital images;
- it provides, on the basis of the above figures, some *quantitative* information about an image quality;
- it exploits such results for automatically computing the optimal sampling ratio preserving, as much as possible, a certain visual characteristics.

3   Modelling Clutter

In this section we present the formal framework that aims at modeling the clutter produced by over-plotting data. For the sake of simplicity, we consider a 2D space in which we plot elements by associating a pixel to each data element; the pixel position is computed mapping two data attributes on the spatial coordinates. As an example, Figure 1 shows about 160,000 mail parcels plotted on the X-Y plane according to their weight (X axis) and volume (Y axis). It is worth noting that, even if the occupation of the screen is very little, the area close to the origin is very crowded (usually parcels are very light and little), so a great number of collisions is present in that area.

Having this scenario in mind and exploiting well known results coming from the calculus of probability, we derive a function that estimates the amount of colliding points and, as a consequence, the amount of free available space. More formally, two points are in collision when their projection is on the same physical pixel (in most cases that happens for rounding issue); free space is the percentage of pixels that is not assigned to any element. In order to derive such a function,

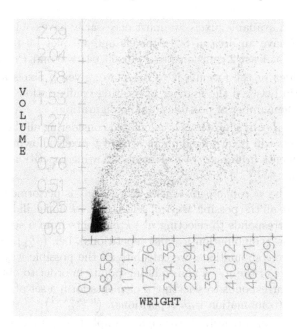

Fig. 1. *Plotting mail parcels*

we imagine to *toss* n data points in a completely random way (that is, the probability for each point to fall on a certain position is constant for any position) on a fixed area of p pixels. This assumption is quite reasonable if we conduct our analysis on *small* areas.

To construct such functions we use a probabilistic model based on the parameters just described, that here we summarize for the sake of clarity:

- n is the number of points we want to plot;
- $p = l \times l$ is the number of available pixels (we are considering square areas);
- k is the number of collisions we are expecting to find;
- d is the number of free pixels we are expecting to find.

The probability of having *exactly* k collisions plotting n points on an area of p pixels, $Pr(k, n, p)$, is given by the following formula:

$$\frac{\binom{p}{n-k}\binom{n-k+k-1}{k}}{\binom{p+n-1}{n}} \text{ if } n \leq p \text{ and } k \in [0, n-1]$$
$$\text{or } n > p \text{ and } k \in [n-p, n-1]$$

$$0 \qquad \text{if } n > p \text{ and } k \in [0, n-p]$$

The function is defined only for $k < n$, because it is impossible to have more collisions than plotted points. Moreover, it is easy to understand that in some cases the probability is equal to zero: if $n > p$, because of we are plotting more points than available pixels, we must necessarily have some collisions. For example, if we have an area of 8×8 pixels and we plot 66 points, we must necessarily have at least 2 collisions, so $Pr(0, 66, 64) = 0$ and $Pr(1, 66, 64) = 0$.

The basic idea of the formula is to calculate, given p pixels and n plotted points, the ratio between the number of existing configurations with *exactly* k collisions and the number of possible total configurations.

The *# of total configurations* is calculated considering all the possible ways in which n points can be arranged on an area of p pixels allowing collisions,i.e., selecting n elements from a set of p elements allowing repetitions (combination with repetitions): $\binom{p+n-1}{n}$.

Calculating the *# config with exactly k collisions* is performed in two steps. We first calculate all the possible ways of selecting $n-k$ non colliding points from p pixels, that corresponds to selecting $n - k$ elements from a set of p elements without collisions, (combination *without* repetitions), i.e., $\binom{p}{n-k}$. After that, for each of the above combinations, we calculate all the possible ways of hitting k times one or more of the $n - k$ non colliding points in order to obtain exactly k collisions, that corresponds to selecting k elements form a set of $n - k$ elements *with* repetitions (combination *with* repetitions): $\binom{n-k+k-1}{k}$.

From this formula we derived, through a simple C program, a series of functions (see Figure 2) showing the behavior of the observed area as the number of plotted points increases. More precisely, we compute the available free pixels d (Y axis, as percentage w.r.t. p), the mean, and deviation of the number of colliding elements k (Y axis, as percentage w.r.t. n) for any given number of plotted points n (X axis, as percentage w.r.t. p). For example, if we have an area of 64 pixels, the graph tell us that plotting 50% (32) of p points we foresee an average of 32.6% (10.4) collisions (variance 4.72). On the other hand, if we plot 32 points having 10.442 collisions we can compute the free pixels d, as $d = 64 - (32 - 10.442) = 42.442$ (66.3%).

The behavior of the functions is quite intuitive: as the number of plotted points n increases the percentage of collisions increases as well while the free space decreases; the rightmost point corresponds to plotting 255 points over 64 pixels (398.4%) that produces 79.9 % (203.68) collisions and, consequently, leaving $d = 64 - (255 - 203.68) = 12.68$ pixels free (19.8%).

Using this graph we can derive several useful and objective indications on the decay of the plotted image. As an example, the graph can tell us how much we are saturating the space or, as a more complex possibility, the way in which the display is able to represent relative densities and how much to sample the data to guarantee a prefixed visualization quality. This result is exploited in the next section and we clarify it through an example. Assume that we are plotting n points on the area A_1 turning on p_1 pixels and $2n$ points on the area A_2 turning on p_2 pixels. In principle, the user should perceive area A_2 as containing more (i.e., twice as many) points as area A_1. Because of the collisions, $p_2 \neq 2p_1$ and as n increases the user initially looses the information that area A_2 contains twice as many points as A_1 and for greater values of n the user is not able to grasp any difference between A_1 and A_2. As a numerical example, if we plot

30 and 60 points on two areas, the pixels turned on in the two areas will be
$30 - 9.355 = 20.645$ and $60 - 28.78 = 31.22$, so the ratio of displayed pixels is
only 1.51; if we plot 50 and 100 points the ratio decreases to 1.38. So, in order
to preserve the visual impression that area A_2 contains twice as many points as
A_1 accepting a decay of 20 per cent we have to sample the data (50 and 100
points) as much as 60 per cent resulting in 20 and 40 points that, once plotted,
turn on 15.42 and 24.8 pixels, i.e., a ratio of 1.608 (20 per cent of decay).

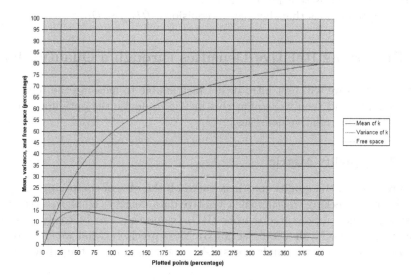

Fig. 2. *Mean and variance of colliding elements*

This is one of the most interesting ways of using the above function: it is
possible to focus on a visual characteristic (e.g., relative density, number of
collisions, screen saturation, etc.) setting a quality threshold and, through the
graph, computing the sampling rate that satisfy such a threshold.

3.1   Real and Represented Densities

The previous results give as a way to control and measure the number of colliding
elements. Before introducing quality metrics and optimization strategies, we need
to clarify our scenario and to introduce new definitions.

We assume the image is displayed on a rectangular area (measured in inches)
and that small squares of area A divide the space in $m \times n$ *sample areas* (SA)
where density is measured. Given a particular monitor, the resolution and size
affect the values used in calculations. In the following we assume that we are
using a monitor of 1280x1024 pixels and size of 13"x10.5". Using these figures
we have 1,310,720 pixels available and if we choose SA of side $l = 0,08$ inch,

the area is covered by 20.480 (128x160) sample areas whose dimension in pixel is 8×8. We consider small areas because of it makes the uniform distribution assumption adopted in Section 3 quite realistic.

For each $SA_{i,j}$, where $1 \le i \le m$ and $1 \le j \le n$, we calculate two different densities : *real data density* (or, shorter, data density) and *represented density*.

Data density is defined as $D_{i,j} = \frac{n_{i,j}}{A}$ where $n_{i,j}$ is the number of data points that fall into sample area $A_{i,j}$.

Represented density is defined as $RD_{i,j} = \frac{p_{i,j}}{A}$ where $p_{i,j}$ is the number of distinct active pixels that fall into $SA_{i,j}$.

It is quite obvious that, because of collisions, $RD_{i,j} \le D_{i,j}$.

4   Preserving Relative Densities through a Quality Metric

In this Section we will first introduce a metric able to measure the represented image quality and then we exploit this metric to devise the optimum sampling factor preserving relative densities.

4.1   The Quality Metric

The provision of the quality metric is based on the idea of comparing couples of sample areas checking whether their relative data density (D) is preserved when considering their represented density (RD) (value that can be easily estimated exploiting the results shown in Section 3). More precisely, what we do is to see if for any given couple of sample areas $SA_{i,j}$ and $SA_{k,l}$ one of the following rules holds:

$$if\ D_{i,j} > D_{k,l}\ then\ RD_{i,j} > RD_{k,l}$$
$$if\ D_{i,j} = D_{k,l}\ then\ RD_{i,j} = RD_{k,l}$$
$$if\ D_{i,j} < D_{k,l}\ then\ RD_{i,j} < RD_{k,l}$$

Introducing the $Diff(x, y)$ function defined as:

$$Diff(x, y) = \begin{cases} 1 & if\ x > y \\ 0 & if\ x = y \\ -1 & if\ x < y \end{cases}$$

we can define the $match(i, j, k, l)$ function that returns true iff $Diff(D_{i,j}, D_{k,l}) = Diff(RD_{i,j}, RD_{k,l})$.

In order to produce a measure, we apply an algorithm that iteratively considers all the possible couples of SAs comparing their D and RD through the $Diff$ function, and counting the number of times it finds a matching pair. The complexity of this algorithm is $O(n^2)$.

At the end the variable *sum* contains the number of matchings encountered during the iterations. Then, dividing it by the total number of possible couples, it gives the percentage of matching sample areas ranging between 1 and 0 (the greater the better).

The quality function permits us to measure the amount of distortion the image presents and to evaluate in objective way the effect of the applied sampling strategies. In the following Section we describe how to use it when uniform sampling is adopted.

4.2   Optimum Sampling Factor

Uniform sampling is an effective technique to deal with cluttered 2d scatter-plots. However it is not clear how to use this technique to reveal the underlying characteristics of data and what is the amount of sampling that should be employed to obtain an adequate visual representation.

Using the quality metric introduced above we can measure, for a given sampling factor, the quality of the generated image and than we can estimate the optimum amount of sampling to apply to produce an ideal final representation.

The idea is to find the maximum value of a function that calculates the quality of the representation for a given amount of sampling. More formally, if s is the *sampling factor* [1] we want to maximize the $SQuality(s)$ function that for each sampling amount returns the quality of the image. It can be thought as a function that samples that underlying data with a sampling amount of s and calculates the quality of the final image with the function $Quality$.

In formulas it can be described as an optimization problem:

$$\begin{cases} max(SQuality(s)) \\ s \in (0, 1] \end{cases}$$

As posed here the problem operates with continuous values of s. Nevertheless, because of very small differences in the amount of sampling does not produce perceivable visual differences, we employ an algorithm that runs considering a fixed number of sampling factors. In our tests we have considered sampling factors with three digits after the decimal point so that the total number of sampling factors tested are 1000 (i.e., $0.001, \ldots, 0.999, 1.000$).

In the following we show an example to clarify our approach. Assume we are plotting 2264 (this strange number comes from a random data generation) points on a screen composed by 400x400 pixels arranged in 100 sample areas of size 4x4 pixels. In the example, to denote the data density and the represented data density we use the number of data elements and the active pixels, respectively, neglecting the SA area value (what we called A), that is just a constant. In Figure 3 (a) the data densities (in terms of number of points) corresponding to each sample area are displayed. In this situation it is possible to compare $100(100-1)/2 = 4950$ distinct pairs of data densities.

Using the formal results coming from Section 3 we can estimate the represented data densities, shown in Figure 3 (b) (in terms of active pixels) and our analysis reports a total of 452 non matching pairs. As a simple example, consider

---

[1] here we consider the sampling factor s as the percentage of data elements randomly extracted from the data source (e.g. $s = 0.1$ means we are extracting 10% of the original data randomly)

46	2	11	25	2	31	19	21	18	2
4	3	12	38	45	49	26	35	12	38
38	38	35	46	28	8	21	42	22	7
35	24	4	2	30	9	41	31	21	23
41	47	45	6	35	2	7	2	38	28
8	4	39	2	28	27	42	22	43	29
2	35	21	39	44	35	2	6	5	25
32	2	31	29	8	28	33	39	5	40
43	4	12	16	23	2	9	48	39	8
11	25	2	46	10	38	2	15	6	19

(a) 4751 perceptible differences

12	2	7	10	2	11	9	9	9	2
3	3	7	11	12	12	10	11	7	11
11	11	11	12	10	6	9	12	10	5
11	10	3	2	11	6	12	11	9	10
12	12	12	5	11	2	5	2	11	10
6	3	12	2	10	10	12	10	12	11
2	11	9	12	12	11	2	5	4	10
11	2	11	11	6	10	11	12	4	12
12	3	7	8	10	2	6	12	12	6
7	10	2	12	6	11	2	8	5	9

(b) 4299 perceptible differences

32	1	7	17	1	21	13	14	12	1
2	2	8	26	31	34	18	24	8	26
26	26	24	32	19	5	14	29	15	4
24	16	2	1	21	6	29	21	14	16
29	33	31	4	24	1	4	1	26	19
5	2	27	1	19	19	29	15	30	20
1	24	14	27	31	24	1	4	3	17
22	1	21	20	5	19	23	27	3	28
30	2	8	11	16	1	6	33	27	5
7	17	1	32	7	26	1	10	4	13

(c)

11	1	5	9	1	9	7	8	7	1
2	2	6	10	11	11	9	10	6	10
10	10	10	11	9	4	8	11	8	3
10	8	2	1	9	5	11	9	8	8
11	11	11	3	10	1	3	1	10	9
4	2	10	1	9	9	11	8	11	9
1	10	8	10	11	10	1	3	3	9
10	1	9	9	4	9	10	10	3	10
11	2	6	7	8	1	5	11	10	4
5	9	1	11	5	10	1	6	3	7

(d) 4360 perceptible differences

Fig. 3. A screen area made of 100 sample areas: real (a) and represented (b) data densities vs sampled (0.71%) real (c) and represented (d) data densities

the sample areas $SA_{1,7}$, $SA_{1,8}$, and $SA_{1,9}$ that, even characterized by different D values (19,21,18), are mapped onto the RD value (9). So, the overall image quality, according to our metric, is (4950-542)/4950= 0.89.

Applying our algorithm we found the optimum sampling factor, 0.708, that produces the new dataset shown in Figure 3 (c) whose estimated representation is in Figure 3(d). The analysis reports a total of 391 non matching pairs. To understand how some differences are rescued, consider again the above three sample areas that, after the sampling, are mapped into three new values (7,8,7) showing that sample area $SA_{1,8}$ is more dense than $SA_{1,7}$ and $SA_{1,9}$ (on the other hand, the difference between $SA_{1,7}$ and $SA_{1,9}$ is still hidden). The new overall image quality is (4950-391)/4950= 0.92.

5   Working Prototype

In order to validate our ideas we have developed a first prototype in Java using OpenGL whose purpose is to provide precise measures about pixel displacement and space usage. The tool operates on pixel basis and takes as input a file containing relational data. Each record element is associated with a pixel and its position is derived from two data fields whose value determines X-axis and Y-axis placement. The visualization pane is divided in N x N sample areas (e.g 8 X 8 pixels) where N can be set by the user.

The user can obtain some interesting information. Some are associated with the partition of the area in sample areas, some others are global information. This information can be extracted by the user in form of a report or, alternatively, it can be explored interactively. In particular, the following pieces of information are available:

- Number of available pixels - it is a constant value and it depends on the size of sample areas (e.g., for 8 x 8 SAs the number of available pixels is 64)
- Number of active pixels - it is the number of pixels within the sample area that are on, an it forms the basis to calculate the represented density
- Overlapping pixels - it is the number of pixels within the sample area that overlap
- Data density - it is the number of data elements that are mapped into the given sample area
- Total number of available pixels
- Total number of active pixels
- Total number of overlapping pixels
- Overall image quality measure
- Best sampling factor

Exploiting our prototype, we applied our technique against the postal parcels shown in Figure 1. In particular we first zoomed on the most crowded area (weigh between 2.16 and 15.7 and volume between 0.01 and 0.03), obtaining the image shown in Figure 4 (a), that contains more than 50,000 parcels (about 30 % of the whole dataset compressed in less than 1 % of the whole screen). After that we applied three different sampling ratios: the optimum (40.31%) computed by our algorithm (Figure 4 (c)), a too strong ratio (10 %) (Figure 4(d)) and a too low ratio (70 %) (Figure 4 (b)). The figure makes quite clear the negative effects of inadequate sampling ratios and validates our quality metric.

6   Conclusion and Future WorK

In this paper we presented a low grain, combinatorial sampling technique that aims at automatically reducing visual clutter in a 2D scatter plot. To the best of our knowledge this approach is a totally novel way of sampling visual data. The technique exploits some statistical results and a formal model describing and measuring over plotting, screen occupation, and both data density and represented data density. Such a model allows for (a) measuring in an objective way the decay of several data characteristics and (b) computing the right amounts of sampling to apply in order to guarantee some quality parameters. In this paper we showed how this technique can effectively preserve relative density.

Several open issues rise from this work:

- users must be involved. Our approach provides precise figures but we need to map them against user perceptions. As an example, still referring to our approach, if a sample area contains twice as many active pixels as another

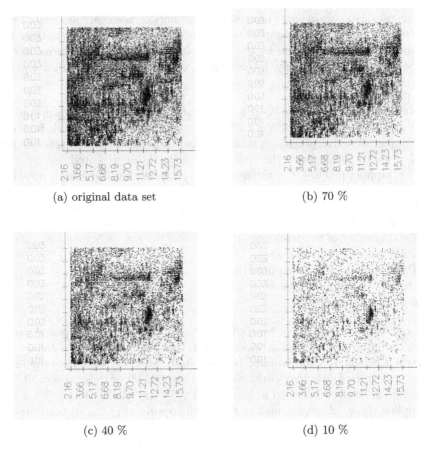

(a) original data set   (b) 70 %

(c) 40 %   (d) 10 %

Fig. 4. Computing the optimal sampling ratio: original data set (a), too low sampling (b), optimal sampling (c), and too strong sampling (d)

one, does the user perceive the feeling of observing a double density for any total occupation of the areas? On the other hand, how much two sample areas may differ in pixel number still giving the user the sensation of having the same data density?

– sampling areas. Several choices deserve more attention: it is our intention to analyze the influence of increasing/decreasing of sampling area dimension, in term of image quality and computational aspects.

We are actually extending the prototype functionalities to apply and verify our ideas. We want to implement a dataset generator to conduct controlled tests. The dataset generator will permit to generate artificial distributions, giving the user the possibility to control specific parameters, that will be used to create specific cases considered critical or interesting. It will be useful to verify the visual effect and to conduct user studies.

7   Acknowledgements

We would like to thank Pasquale Di Tucci for his invaluable help in implementing the software prototype.

References

[1] Christopher Ahlberg and Ben Shneiderman. Visual information seeking: tight coupling of dynamic query filters with starfield displays. In *Proceedings of the CHI conference*, pages 313–317. ACM Press, 1994.

[2] Benjamin B. Bederson and James D. Hollan. Pad++: a zooming graphical interface for exploring alternate interface physics. In *Proceedings of the UIST ACM symposium*, pages 17–26. ACM Press, 1994.

[3] G. Ellis and A. Dix. Density control through random sampling: an architectural perspective. In *Proceedings of Conference on Information Visualisation*, pages 82–90, July 2002.

[4] G. W. Furnas. Generalized fisheye views. In *Proceedings of the CHI conference*, pages 16–23. ACM Press, 1986.

[5] Alexander Hinneburg, Daniel A. Keim, and Markus Wawryniuk. Hd-eye: visual clustering of high dimensional data. In *Proceedings of the 2002 ACM SIGMOD international conference on Management of data*, pages 629–629. ACM Press, 2002.

[6] B. Johnson and B. Shneiderman. Tree-maps: A space-filling approach to the visual-ization of hierarchical information structures. In *Proceedings of IEEE Visualization*, pages 284–291, October 1991.

[7] Daniel A. Keim. Designing pixel-oriented visualization techniques: Theory and applications. *IEEE Transactions on Visualization and Computer Graphics*, 6(1):59–78, 2000.

[8] John Lamping and Ramana Rao. Visualizing large trees using the hyperbolic browser. In *Conference companion on Human factors in computing systems*, pages 388–389. ACM Press, 1996.

[9] Nancy Miller, Beth Hetzler, Grant Nakamura, and Paul Whitney. The need for metrics in visual information analysis. In *Proceedings of the 1997 workshop on New paradigms in information visualization and manipulation*, pages 24–28. ACM Press, 1997.

[10] Brath Richard. Concept demonstration: Metrics for effective information visualization. In *Proceedings For IEEE Symposium On Information Visualization*, pages 108–111. IEEE Service Center, Phoenix, AZ, 1997.

[11] T. C. Sprenger, R. Brunella, and M. H. Gross. H-blob: a hierarchical visual clustering method using implicit surfaces. In *Proceedings of the conference on Visualization '00*, pages 61–68. IEEE Computer Society Press, 2000.

[12] Edward R. Tufte. *The visual display of quantitative information*. Graphics Press, 1986.

[13] Allison Woodruff, James Landay, and Michael Stonebraker. Constant density visualizations of non-uniform distributions of data. In *Proceedings of the 11th annual ACM symposium on User interface software and technology*, pages 19–28. ACM Press, 1998.

[14] Allison Woodruff, James Landay, and Michael Stonebraker. Vida: (visual information density adjuster). In *CHI '99 extended abstracts on Human factors in computing systems*, pages 19–20. ACM Press, 1999.

A View on Views

Ariel Shamir

The Interdisciplinary Center, Herzliya
(arik@idc.ac.il)

Abstract. This paper presents an intelligent interface for a personal information management system. The system addresses two main deficiencies in personal information retrieval: the cluttering of information in interfaces which creates difficulties finding data and concentrating on a specific task, and the scattering of related information across different applications and locations. The system design uses the notion of a view which is extremely versatile as an additional level of abstraction above the file system, the folders, and the desktop. A view defines the context of a specific task or subject, and can include and display information according to subjective ordering of relevancy. Semantic information is gathered in an attribute database using a novel attribute delegation mechanism which constantly augments the items with attribute information.

1 Introduction

Most personal computing devices such as PCs, laptops and PDAs today have a graphical user interface of which main purpose is to convey the device's functionality. However, these devices are used for multiple purposes such as business-oriented tasks, personal activities, educational tasks, and even everyday chores. Most of those are highly dependent on information stored on the device in different places and in different formats. The consequence of such multi-functionality is very often chaotic and over crowded interfaces and file systems (see Figure 1). A common user spends a lot of time opening and switching between applications in pursuit of data and files related to the same subject. It is difficult to locate the relevant information to perform a specific task, and it is difficult to concentrate only on the relevant information.

Numerous researchers and companies have recognized this situation and suggested different solutions such as smart search engines; better file system designs or new graphic interfaces for navigation (see related work section for review). Nevertheless, in this paper we claim that two distinct problems are combined in practice to create this situation. The first which we term **scattering** is related to storage and information retrieval, and the second which we term **cluttering** is related to the graphical interface. While previous work tends to concentrate on solving scattering [20, 5, 7] or cluttering [9, 8, 1], we suggest a solution which addresses both:

1. **Scattering:** means information related to a specific task is distributed in different locations, across different applications, supporting different types (emails, documents, spreadsheets, presentations etc.) and possibly even stored on different devices.

A. Butz et al. (Eds.): SG 2004, LNCS 3031, pp. 90–100, 2004.
© Springer-Verlag Berlin Heidelberg 2004

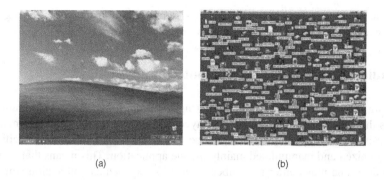

(a)   (b)

Fig. 1. Example of (somewhat exaggerated) cluttering of information: a PC desktop when we begin using our computer (left) and after a while (right).

2. **Cluttering:** means irrelevant information is often distracting the view or search, making it difficult to concentrate on a specific task or to find data requested.

Although the graphic aspect of this work can be considered basic, we believe it is also fundamental. This is due to considering the primal everyday usage of computing-device interfaces and suggesting how the definition of smart graphical user interfaces should be approached in an information-rich environment.

The key notion in our system is the view. A view can be seen as a workspace (such as a desktop) or a briefcase (such as a folder) where you gather all information related to a specific subject or task in one place. This can be considered as "wearing a different hat" each time you use a different view on your device. A view can include different types of information such as documents, emails, web-pages, images and applications (see Figure 5). In this sense, a view can be seen as a subjective gateway to your data, creating an application-free interface. Its versatility and numerous tasks will be discussed below. A somewhat simplified conceptualization of a view is to consider it an additional level of abstraction over the file-system in the same manner the file-system is an abstraction over disk sectors.

Current trends in OS development (see e.g. Microsoft new system code named Longhorn) and extensions to the world wide web (the Semantic Web initiative [12]) depend on the definition of attributes and resources as meta information. Similarly, a unified attribute database for information and data is the basis on which our solution is built. Nevertheless, our solution is geared more towards personal and subjective semantics or preferences, and it is unique in the way the database is built and in the way it is accessed and used. To build the database we use an intelligent attribute delegation mechanism which constantly augments the database with descriptive information even for non-textual data. This can be seen as an agent which finds relations based on *subjective* context of the data according to its usage and not only based on its content. To access the database we believe that the use of explicit search queries should be limited. Instead, we employ implicit querying by creating and displaying a context-dependent order on data from relevant to irrelevant. Although not eliminating it altogether, this order reduces the need for searching and querying.

In the next few sections we describe our system in a bottom up approach: beginning from the attribute database and working up towards the views.

2   Building Semantics: an Attribute Database

The main reason for scattering and cluttering in current interfaces on computing devices is the way data is handled and displayed. Most access to data and information is location-based and application-oriented. Each data item is classified into a specific type and recognized and manipulated mainly by one application. This means that to access or find data, one must either remember its position or open an application which can help locate it. Often each application holds its own database with its own unique format (emails, web-bookmarks, documents etc.) creating redundancy in similar but separate information structures, databases and hierarchies. This results in even larger inconsistencies and scattering [6].

Our approach for information management is defined by concentrating on the subject or task that the user is performing, and defining its context using a view. This approach is based on the assumption that the amount of data relevant to a specific task or subject is much smaller than all the data stored on the device. Furthermore, a specific piece of information can be relevant to more than one task. Using semantics can reduce searching significantly and allow natural access to the data from numerous contexts.

The core of our system is an indexing database of data items. A *data item* (DI) can be defined as any piece of information enriched with attributes which is entered into the database. In practice we include files, folders, applications, emails, and URLs in our database. Entering DIs to the database is performed by attaching attributes to them either manually or automatically using software agents. The database does not contain the actual DIs but only the attribute-set of each DI with a link to the position of the actual item. Once DIs including attributes are stored inside the database, queries can be used to examines the database and retrieve subsets of DIs as results (Figure 2).

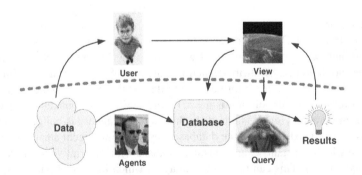

Fig. 2. An overview of our system: at the base, a database engine creates semantics by utilizing agents to attach attributes to the data and establish relevancy by performing queries. However from a user perspective all interface to data and information is done through views.

An attribute of a DI can be any type of information which can characterize a DI. In our system a DI is described by a pair: `<attribute name : value>`. This scheme supports many meta-data description systems and can benefit from their use. Some conventional attributes include: type, size, author, creation time and modification time. The main question in any information system depending on attributes is how to extract and augment the data items with attributes? One cannot depend on users to tediously add attributes to each and every data item. Many information systems turn to automatic indexing and extraction techniques. With the advent of the World Wide Web such indexing algorithms are a fertile field of research. Nevertheless, turning to personal information and data there are some limitations to general automatic algorithms:

1. Most of the automatic indexing algorithms work on text. However, many data items such as images, media files, applications, and graphics files (e.g. in hard disks and not on web sites) cannot be indexed easily by text extraction tools.
2. Even in text documents, there are keywords or phrases which do not appear in the text content, but are still relevant to the data item.
3. There are many relations between data items and words or phrases which are *subjective* and cannot be identified using universal language dictionaries.

To address these limitations, and also to relieve the user from exhaustive manual tagging, we devise a subjective delegation scheme which can propagate attributes to relevant data items. The scheme uses views as *subjective* contexts to delegate related attributes to any data item, be it textual or non-textual, which is added or used inside a view. The delegation uses a special field-type called `tags` where each DI can simply hold many strings. Tags simplify automatic attribute extraction for both software agents and manual insertion. Although tags describe DIs, the user does not have to add tags to each and every DI. Instead, from the user perspective, tags are attributes of the *view*. When a user creates a new view for a task or subject, she can augment it with several tags and keywords related to the task. This becomes a more feasible effort (see Figure 4). Once several items are placed inside a view, an automatic agent can search for more common words or phrases in the context of this view and enriches the set of tags of the view [3]. Every new DI, be it textual or non-textual, that is added to the view automatically inherits all the view tags both subjective and objective.

Using this scheme relieves the above limitations: 1. Non-textual DIs are enriched with tags if they are inserted and used in a view. 2. The tags and phrases originate from the context of the view and not only from the content of the specific DI, and 3. The tags can include words and phrases inserted by the user representing his own subjective relevancy point of view.

3   Using Semantics: Relevancy Ordering

An average user of a computing device is exposed to huge amounts and diversity of data. Current interfaces and information management applications either let the user order the information in a hierarchical manner, or use queries to search and find information.

A hierarchy is indeed a natural and effective structure for humans to organize information. Nevertheless, hierarchies are effective mostly when they remain small. Today, desktop computers may include thousands of folders, and web browsers can include hundreds of favorite internet sites and addresses. Navigation becomes increasingly difficult in such large hierarchies. Furthermore, in their basic use, hierarchies are rigid structures: each item has a single position and a single path from the root. In order to access this item one must remember this path and follow it exactly. Solutions used to convert the rigid structure into a DAG (soft links or shortcuts) are usually cumbersome. In contrast, using views a specific data item can reside in many views regardless of its actual location, creating a highly connected interface to the stored information.

Queries are used when data is buried in the hierarchy or there is a need to search for items in vast unknown repositories (libraries, the web). It seems extraordinary that one would have to use queries or search engines to find ones own data; unfortunately, this is often the case in current systems. In order to gain a sense of control over personal data, we advocate the use of subjective relevancy. Using a specific context, we classify all data items into three categories: THIS DATA, RELEVANT DATA, and OTHER DATA (see Figure 3). Scattering and cluttering give the feeling that we always have to search hard in the huge hierarchies of all OTHER DATA for the RELEVANT DATA and even for THIS DATA. Smart search utilities give tools to extract information using explicit queries. However, these can become quite complicated to use, or have an unfriendly or insufficient user interface. Instead, the use of views supports an implicit decomposition of data where THIS DATA is almost at our fingertips, the RELEVANT DATA is close-by, and all OTHER DATA is hidden but accessible.

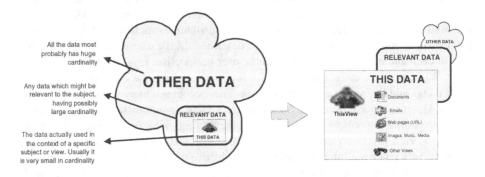

Fig. 3. Gaining control over your data by grouping and ordering it according to relevancy. Instead of constantly navigating or searching for your data in huge irrelevant amounts (left), a view puts the data you most use in context near-by, the relevant data close-by, and all other data is hidden behind (right).

In order to create the ordering of data items in a specific context (i.e. view), there is a need for a relevancy-measure of data items to views. Since this measure must apply to any data-item of any type and nature, textual and non-textual, and in different *subjective* contexts, it cannot use only the DI's content. Instead, we use the attributes characterizing the DIs to define relevancy. Let T represent the set of all tags in the system, and PT the power set of T (the set of all subsets of T), we define a relevancy measure as a function $f : PT \times PT \rightarrow R$. Specifically, a measure compares the set of tags defined in the view with the set of tags defined in the DI and returns a numerical value. Higher values represent higher relevancy of a given DI to a given view. When used in a specific view, all relevancy value for all DIs are normalized and sorted to create the relevancy list.

Since the DIs may include multiple tags from various views of which the DI is a part of, a simple comparison of tags is not sufficient. There are numerous ways to define the relevancy measure f based on the set of tags, and we have tested several options [3]. Currently, we use a composite measure by grouping the tags into three levels. The most important or most specific description tags are placed in level 1, and the least important or most general in level 3. Automatic extraction agents can add tags to a each level according to its generality. Furthermore, the user may insert, delete or move tags from any level in a view (see Figure 4). The relevancy of each DI to a specific view is a weighted sum of the tags matched in each level separately. Normalizing this measure to [0,1] and sorting inside a view leads to the separation between RELEVANT DATA, which are items that have high relevancy measure and OTHER DATA which are items which have low relevancy measure (below a certain threshold). THIS DATA are all the DIs that were actually inserted into the view by the user.

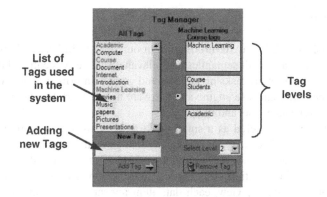

Fig. 4. The tagging manager interface makes it simple to add keywords and phrases to describe the subjective context of a view in three different levels.

We have tested this relevancy measure in several contexts. We start with a small seed of tags relevant to some subjective context and add DIs to define the view context. Next, we use this set of tags and order other data-items not contained in the view to create the relevancy list. The list always contains some false-positive data item examples. Nevertheless, in order to measure its effectiveness we examined the difference between the relevancy-measure value and values assigned by a human user to the 50 most relevant data items in the list. In table 1 we show the average absolute difference of these measures in several contexts. As these examples illustrate, one can find a high correlation between the two measures. It seems that such a relevancy measure can in fact lead to an effective partial ordering of data items in the context of a given view.

context	c1	c2	c3	c4
Using 10 DIs in THIS DATA	0.317	0.328	0.431	0.601
Using 50 DIs in THIS DATA	0.331	0.488	0.425	0.513

Table 1. Average absolute difference between manual relevancy and measured relevancy, scaled to [0-1]. The differences depend on many parameters such as the number of items defining the context in the view (shown here as two rows in the table), the set of data items used for ordering, the set of tags created, and more (details can be found in [3]).

Sometimes the relevancy lists can still become too large for browsing. This is often because they include many small items which are less important in general, but are still relevant to the specific context (e.g. many compilation files or debugging files or log files in a software project, or small gif pictures or icons in a web project). More focused results can be achieved by filtering the relevancy list or using regular queries inside the list. Such searches and queries will be more manageable since the lists are already constrained to include relevant items, and are more focused in the context of the specific view.

4   The View

The view is the main gateway to information in our system. In fact, as Figure 2 illustrates, the user interface to all semantics and relevancy can be concentrated in views. A user creates views for many tasks or subjects and gathers information onto them. Only behind the scene, the database engine and software agents work to augment data with tags and create relevancy lists and links.

A view can be considered as a small desktop, as a folder, as a project or as an interface to a query. It is exactly this versatility that gives the view-idiom its power. A view is represented as a window which is a workspace onto which the user can drag or add any type of information such as files, folders, applications, emails and URLs (Figure 5). Once inside the view, each data-item appears as a small icon similar to the known symbols and idioms inside a folder or on a desktop. A user can also create groupings of items. As a workspace, gathering all types of data and applications related to a specific subject into one view reduces the scattering effect in usual computing environments. Since views include only items related to a specific task or subject, they also reduce the cluttering effect abundant in current interfaces.

When a user opens a specific view, an automatic mechanism can open pre-selected applications or data items (e.g. development environments, edited documents, web-sites or emails) for fast accessing. This means a view can define and setup a complete working environment composed of all the data related to a specific project and all the applications needed to perform the tasks involved in the project.

The implicit relevancy measure defined by the tags of the view creates the context or point-of-view to create the relevancy list. The user can display or hide the relevancy list as a portion of the view window (Figure 5). The user can browse through it, narrow it down by using additional filtering or explicit querying, and drag items from the list

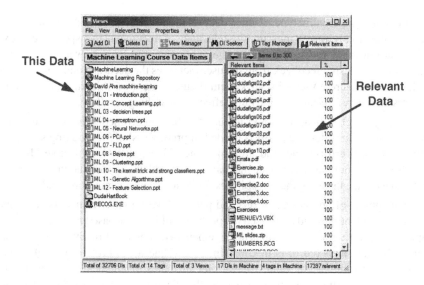

Fig. 5. Inside a specific view, THIS DATA includes files, urls, emails and applications related to this view, and the RELEVANT DATA is displayed as an ordered list of many possibly related items. The user can browse through the list of relevant items and drag items to the left section of the view. This will make these items part of THIS DATA. The user may also select items (emails, URLS, files, folders) from outside the view and drag them inside.

into the view, moving it into THIS DATA. Hence, a view provides a simple and natural interface for semantic querying and searching of data.

The views system co-exists with the regular OS hierarchies and access system. It does not rename or change files or folders positions, storing only links to the actual data. In an ideal situation all data access, creation and saving would be performed inside views without regard to where the data is actually stored. The current situation may leads to some synchronization and duality problems. To overcome such problems, we have used 'soft-links' to DIs, and indicate a missing link by a special icon. This allows the user to restore the location of the data item in a view or delete it.

5   Related Work

Indexing of files using keywords, creating a database and providing a search engine using queries and relevance scores is a well known scheme used from early days of information retrieval [18] and up to current day web searches [15, 16, 2]. Nevertheless, the problem dealt in our work is distinctly different due to the subjective nature of the data and access patterns. There are numerous methods for indexing and searching, however they mostly concentrate on text-based contents. One of the main challenges of attribute-based systems is the difficulty to gather attribute fields [14]. Recent work [19] suggests that inter-data relations will be used for automating attribute extraction. Our system defines exactly this type of inter-data relation using views and relevancy. Another key question is how to measure the relevancy of documents in a specific context? Traditional relevancy measure relies on the data content [13]. However, studies such as [22] show that using feedback from the user increases the accuracy and effectiveness of relevancy measures. Views in our system define context for this kind of subjective measures and therefore can provide more effective searching results.

Indexing and classification of non-textual data (e.g. multi-media) is a difficult problem on its own. Considerable effort is needed in preprocessing for indexing such data. Methods are still error-prone, and are not context-dependent or subjective [10, 21]. Towards this end our tag-inheritance mechanism can add context textual information to non-textual data, enhancing the possibilities for better relevancy measures and retrieval.

In the context of operating systems and personal working environments, a number of works have identified and addressed the problems of location based file accessing and simple tree-based hierarchies for data arrangement [4]. Semantic File Systems [11] used regular OS commands (cd or ls in Unix) instead of queries to browse through virtual directories constraining the values of various attributes of all files. Some works try and solve the scattering problem by using synchronization mechanisms. Synchronizing URL, email and document hierarchies in one computer [5, 6], synchronizing across multiple storage devices by creating a centralized but portable database of all documents and attributes [20], or managing URLs using flexible hierarchies [7]. Nevertheless, these systems solve a portion of the problem and do not address data accessing and searching.

There are a number of systems which advocate associative or property-based access to data instead of location based. These systems are usually supported by an indexing scheme, a database and queries. Recent press releases also indicate that Microsoft's new OS (longhorn) will add relational database capabilities to the file system (NTFS) to support better search and querying. Nevertheless it is still difficult to imagine how semantic attributes will be gathered and subjective contexts used. In LifeStreams [9] (which evolved to a commercial system), as well as in [17], information is organized according to a timeline. Overall these systems are more similar to an enhanced search engine than to a workspace. Presto [8] advocates property based access for place-less documents. Using graphical interface the user can create collections of documents by constraining their attributes, in effect creating a query. Similar to our scheme, a document in Presto can be a part of many collections. However, there is no separation between items actually used in the collection and items only relevant to the collection. HayStack [1] intent was to provide the user with a flexible environment to define whichever arrangements of, and views of information they find most effective.

Nevertheless, subjective semantics is not used and indexing concentrates mainly on textual data. In general, the models for displaying dynamic information structures such as streams in LifeStreams, Virtual directories in Semantic file systems and collections in Presto, allow context sensitive and flexible arrangements of data, but must be supported by active querying. In contrast, our notion of views is much more stable and the user does not have to use queries in order to create semantic sub-sets of data. Furthermore, the collection of data items inserted into a view stays stable: the separation between working documents (THIS DATA) and related documents (RELEVANT DATA) creates a more natural and effective interface for the user.

6 Summary

This work presents the design and implementation of an interface to a personal information management system which is based on subjective semantics. Using views, which define specific contexts, one can reduce the cluttering and scattering of current user interfaces and file systems. Views can be defined to be as specific as a course assignment, or a particular artist's music, or as general as a whole course or as a library of all images stored on a device.

The basis for such a semantic system is the use of a database of attributes describing the data items. However, our solution frees the user from the need to tag each data item in use. The user only adds descriptive tags to views which define the specific context. Using automatic augmentation of tags and delegation of tags, the system is able to propagate semantic information in an effective manner, and also separate between relevant and less relevant data.

In future work we hope to enhance both the semantic as well as the graphical side of the system. We are working on finding better relevancy measures based on tags. We are looking at different possible ways to display the relevancy list in a more efficient manner, by quantizing it to groups of similar items or displaying it in a hierarchical manner. Due to the focused content, such hierarchies will remain small and effective for use. Furthermore, the same item can be a part of different hierarchies in different views bypassing the rigid structure of current location-based access systems. Other visual metaphors could be used to display both THIS DATA inside the view and the RELEVANT DATA in the lists. Many user interface issues must also be studied while using such a system. Lastly, we hope to utilize the semantic information gathered using the views system to generally help and create more intelligent behaviors in the interaction between people and computing devices.

7 Acknowledgments

The author would like to thank Guy Romem, Inon Zukerman, Oren Wiezman and Ilan Asayag of the interdisciplinary center for their assistance in implementation and discussion.

References

[1] Eytan Adar, David Karger, and Lynn Stein. Haystack: Per-user information environments. In *Proceedings of CIKM '99*, pages 413–422, Kansas City, MO, 1999. ACM Press.

[2] Arvind Arasu, Junghoo Cho, Hector Garcia-Molina, Andreas Paepcke, and Sriram Raghavan. Searching the web. *ACM Transactions on Internet Technology*, 1(1):2 43, August 2001.

[3] Ilan Assayag and Ariel Shamir. Relevancy measures based on string tags. Technical Report TR-CS-2004-02, The Interdisciplinary Center, 2004.

[4] D. Barreau and B. Nardi. Finding and reminding: File organization from the desktop. *SIGCHI Bulletin*, 27(3):39–43, 1995.

[5] Richard Boardman. Workspaces that work: towards unified personal information management. In *HCI2002 Doctoral Consortium, in Proceedings of HCI2002, People and Computers XVI - Memorable yet Invisible*, volume 2, pages 216–217, London, 2002.

[6] Richard Boardman, Robert Spence, and Martina Angela Sasse. Too many hierarchies? the daily struggle for control of the workspace. In *Proc. HCI International 2003*, pages 216–217, Crete, Greece, 2003.

[7] James Chen, Shawn Wolfe, and Stephen D. Wragg. A distributed multi-agent system for collaborative information management and sharing. In *Proceedings of the 2000 International Conference on Information and Knowledge Management (CIKM'00)*, pages 382–388, McLean, VA, November 2000.

[8] Paul Dourish, W. Keith Edwards, Anthony LaMarca, and Michael Salisbury. Using properties for uniform interaction in the presto document system. In *Proceedings of the ACM Symposium on User Interface Software and Technology (UIST'99)*, pages 55–64. ACM Press, 1999.

[9] Scott Fertig, Eric Freeman, and David Gelernter. Lifestreams: An alternative to the desktop metaphor. In *Proc. CHI96*.

[10] Thomas Funkhouser, Patrick Min, Misha Kazhdan, Joyce Chen, Alex Halderman, David Dobkin, and David Jacobs. A search engine for 3d models. *ACM Transactions on Graphics*, 22(1):83–105, January 2003.

[11] D. K. Gifford, P. Jouvelot, M. A. Sheldon, and J. W. OToole Jr. Semantic file systems. *Operating Systems Review*, 25(5):16–25, 1991.

[12] James Hendler, Tim Berners-Lee, and Eric Miller. Integrating applications on the semantic web. *Journal of the Institute of Electrical Engineers of Japan*, 122(10):676–680, October 2002.

[13] Kalervo Jrvelin and Jaana Keklinen. IR evaluation methods for retrieving highly relevant documents. In *Proceedings of the 23rd annual international ACM SIGIR conference on Research and development in information retrieval*, pages 41 – 48, Athens, Greece, 2000.

[14] Robert J. Kuhns. A survey of information retrieval vendors. Technical Report TR-96-56, Sun Microsystems Laboratories, Mountain View, CA, October 1996.

[15] Steve Lawrence and C. Lee Giles. Searching the world wide web. *Science*, 280(5360):98–100, 1998.

[16] Alberto O. Mendelzon, George A. Mihaila, and Tova Milo. Querying the world wide web. *Int. J. on Digital Libraries*, 1(1):54–67, 1997.

[17] J. Rekimoto. Timescape: A time machine for the desktop environment. In *Late Breaking Papers Proceedings of the ACM SIGCHI Conference on Human Factors in Computing Systems HCI'99*.

[18] G. Salton and M. E. Lesk. Computer evaluation of indexing and text processing. *journal of the ACM*, 15(1):8–36, January 1968.

[19] Craig A. N. Soules and Gregory R. Ganger. Why can't I find my files? new methods for automating attribute assignment. In *Proceedings of the Ninth Workshop on Hot Topics in Operating systems*. USENIX Association, May 2003.

[20] Edward Swierk, Emre Kiciman, Nathan C. Williams, Takashi Fukushima, Hideki Yoshida, Vince Laviano, and Mary Baker. The roma personal metadata service. *Mobile Networks and Applications*, 7(5):407–418, October 2002.

[21] R.C. Veltkamp and M. Tanase. A survey of content-based image retrieval systems. In *Content-based image and video retrieval*, pages 47–101. Kluwer Academic Publishers, 2002.

[22] Ryen W. White, Joemon M. Jose, and Ian Ruthven. A system using implicit feedback and top ranking sentences to help users find relevant web documents. In *25th Annual International ACM SIGIR Conference on Research and Development in Information Retrieval (SIGIR 2002)*, pages 11–15, Tampere, Finland, August 2002.

Floating Labels: Applying Dynamic Potential Fields for Label Layout

Knut Hartmann, Kamran Ali, and Thomas Strothotte

Department of Simulation and Graphics
Otto-von-Guericke University of Magdeburg
Universitätsplatz 2, D-39106 Magdeburg, Germany
{hartmann, kamran, tstr}@isg.cs.uni-magdeburg.de

Abstract. This paper introduces a new method to determine appealing place-ments of textual annotations for complex-shaped geometric models. It employs dynamic potential fields, which consider attractive and repulsive forces between pictorial elements and their textual labels. Several label candidates are computed and evaluated according to weighted penalty functions. The individual weights can be adjusted according to global design decisions or user preferences. More-over, the user can re-arrange individual labels whereas the system re-adjusts the remaining labels. The method is demonstrated by the FLOATING LABEL system.

1 Introduction

A wide range of different application domains benefit from providing natural language explanations for pictorial elements. Frequently, they contain the denotation or unknown technical terms and are thus crucial to establish co-referential relations between picto-rial and textual expressions. The relation between pictorial elements and their associ-ated textual labels is indicated by meta-graphical objects such as connecting lines and anchor points placed on top of pictorial elements.

This concept is very attractive for interactive multi-modal information systems (e.g., ZOOM ILLUSTRATOR [15], ILLUSTRATIVE SHADOWS [16]). In these systems two- or three-dimensional geometric objects are associated with a set of labels. The content to be presented within labels depends on the interaction context and therefore its size changes dynamically. An appealing label layout has to balance various optimal criteria, and should be adjustable to superior design decisions. This paper develops a new tech-nique to layout textual labels for complex-shaped geometric models, which balances various evaluation criteria and is easily adjustable.

We collected a corpus of illustrations with many textual labels, extracted from anatomic textbooks, anatomic atlases, pictorial dictionaries, and technical documentations (e.g., [7, 17, 5]). In a manual analysis we made some simple observations:

1. Labels should be placed near to their reference objects in order to prevent co-referential mismatches. They could be either placed within or outside their ref-erence objects (internal vs. external placement).
2. The length of the line connecting label and pictorial element should be minimized.
3. The connecting line should be orthogonal to a main axis.

A. Butz et al. (Eds.): SG 2004, LNCS 3031, pp. 101–113, 2004.
© Springer-Verlag Berlin Heidelberg 2004

4. Crossings between connecting lines should be prevented.
5. The placement of the anchor point should ease the identification of the pictorial element.
6. In dynamic environments the label placement has to be coherent, i.e., the label position in time $i+1$ should be near to its position in time i.

The central idea to formalize these requirements is to establish positive and negative fields, which induce attractive and repulsive forces between pictorial elements and associated labels. This strategy is known as the *artificial potential field method*. Section 2 introduces this method. Section 3 formalizes the above observations in terms of attractive and repulsive forces, which are also exploited to evaluate various label placement candidates. Section 4 presents our initial results, and Section 5 discusses extensions. Finally, by analyzing related work in Section 6, Section 7 summarizes the new contributions of this work.

2   Potential Fields

Artificial potential fields have been introduced in Robotics by KHATIB [9] and became popular in other fields of Artificial Intelligence. They are inspired by attractive and repulsive forces between electric particles. Therefore, the terms (electric) potential, and its first derivative, the (electric) field, are used.

The classical textbook on robot motion planning by LATOMBE [10] contains a popular formalization, where attractors are modeled as global minima and retractors as maxima within the potential field. The algorithm calculates attractive and repulsive forces for each possible position p for a robot on a plane in a static environment. The attractive force steers the robot in the direction of the target:

$$U_{attr}(p) = c_1 \rho_{goal}^2(p)$$

where $\rho_{goal}(p)$ denotes the minimal distance from p to the target and c_1 is a scaling factor. Moreover, for each obstacle B_i a repulsive force is established:

$$U_{B_i}(p) = \begin{cases} c_2(\frac{1}{\rho_i(p)} - \frac{1}{\rho_0})^2 & , \rho_i(p) \leq \rho_0 \\ 0 & , \rho_i(p) > \rho_0 \end{cases}$$

where $\rho_i(p)$ denotes the minimal distance of p to the obstacle B_i, ρ_0 the spatial influence of the obstacle, and c_2 is another scaling factor. The artificial potential field is defined as the sum of the attractive and all repulsive forces:

$$U(p) = U_{attr} + \sum_i U_{B_i}$$

The algorithm determines the forces at the initial position of the robot and iteratively redirects the robot according to the field F until it reaches a minimum within the potential field. Therefore, gradients $\vec{\nabla}$ of the potential field U on the position p are computed:

$$\vec{F} = -\vec{\nabla}U(p)$$

Throughout this paper we will refer to the objects, which float according to these forces as *particles*. Real applications often employ grid-based space quantization. The challenge in all these applications is to prevent those particles getting stuck within local minima without reaching the global minima.

3   The Floating Labels System

Some of the observations stated in Section 1 can be reformulated in terms of attractive and repulsive forces. Figure 1 depicts several forces, which form the basis of our FLOATING LABELS algorithm:

A: An attractive force between a pictorial element and its associated label,
B: a repulsive force at the object boundary (i.e., the label should be placed entirely within or outside its reference object),
C: a repulsive force between the label and all other pictorial elements,
D: repulsive forces between labels and the image boundary, and
E: repulsive forces between labels.

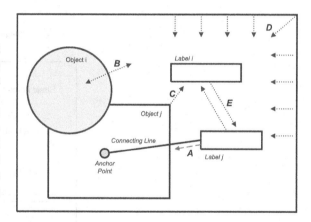

Fig. 1. The force system used by the FLOATING LABELS algorithm. Thick lines denote pictorial elements, associated labels and meta-graphical symbols (anchor points and connecting line). Dashed lines indicate attractive forces, and dotted lines show repulsive forces.

The formalization of potential fields in the previous section is based on the assumption of a single attractive force and constant repulsive forces. In contrast, the FLOATING LABELS system induces a potential field for each individual geometric object and its associated label and assumes dynamic floating labels, inducing dynamic repulsive forces. Note that the Forces A–D remain constant irrespective of the label configuration, whereas Force E is sensitive to the label configuration.

The *static potential field*, i.e., the accumulated attractive and repulsive Forces A–D, is used to determine a set of label placement candidates. Therefore, the algorithm inserts some label particles in the potential field, which then move according to the field F. To expand this point-feature label abstraction, the algorithm determines an area which contains the particle's position and which minimizes the accumulated potential over the label's area. The FLOATING LABELS algorithm considers the label's center and corners. After estimating the best candidates, the overlappings between these labels are resolved in the second phase. In the following we will present the architecture of the FLOATING LABELS system and the formalization of the various attractive and repulsive forces.

3.1   System Architecture

Figure 2 illustrates the architecture of the FLOATING LABELS system. In order to support the integration of various applications, a domain expert establishes the connection between geometric objects and terms in natural language. The domain expert contains or collects all information which is required to establish and exploit multi-modal co-referential relations. The FLOATING LABELS provides advices about an appealing label layout.

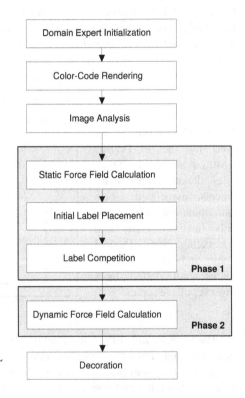

Fig. 2. Architecture of FLOATING LABEL system.

The FLOATING LABELS algorithm is based on color-coded projections of the scene displayed in a 3D application. Therefore, a color-code renderer informs the domain expert about the color encoding scheme, so that the color values could be used to determine visible objects and to retrieve the label's content.

The image analysis extracts the parameters required to compute the static potential field. The initial label placement determines the start positions of label particles, which then float to reach minima within the potential field. These point-feature label abstractions are then expanded to area features and evaluated according to a number of penalty functions. The best label placement candidates are then re-adjusted according to the dynamic potential field. Finally, the label coordinates are sent to the application and rendered (decoration).[1]

3.2   Image Analysis

Based on color-coded projections, the image analyzer determines visible objects. Due to occlusions, the projections of cohesive objects might be split into several segments. For each pictorial element the image analysis creates a list of all segments, their extent, size, and an internal point.

Determination of Internal Points: The placement of the anchor point is crucial to establish the co-referential relation between a pictorial element and its label. Independent from the geometric properties of the reference object, an anchor point has to be placed within the pictorial element. For convex objects, the center of mass is a good candidate. However, the segments could have arbitrary shapes and may contain holes. Therefore, we use a *thinning* algorithm [13], which iteratively shrinks the segment and stops as the segment completely disappears. The last collapsed pixel is the most internal one and is selected as anchor point. This location is furthest away from the silhouette and lies inside the thickest region. This guarantees that the anchor point is placed at a visual dominant region. We will refer to this point within an object O as *interia(O)*.

An analysis of the label layout of hand-made illustrations in our corpus reveals that frequently only one segment is labeled, i.e., only one pair of meta-graphical objects (anchor point, connecting line) establishes the co-referential relation between the pictorial element and its associated label. Currently, the anchor point is placed on an internal point of the biggest visible segment. However, the results of our first experiments suggest to use the segment with the minimal distance to the textual label.

3.3   Static Force Field Calculation

For each object a separate potential field is constructed, considering the object's area as an attractive field (Force A) and the area occupied by all other objects as repulsive force (Force C). Moreover, long-distance attractive forces ensure that each label is directed towards the center of the largest segment of the reference object.

A Laplacian edge detector is applied on the color-coded image. A repulsive function U_{silh} aims at placing the labels either within or outside their reference objects (Force B). Another repulsive function U_{wall} considers the minimal distance to the image borders, in order to prevent labels from leaving the image (Force D). Both repulsive functions need not to be recomputed for specific label configurations. In the following we will present the attractive and repulsive functions employed in the FLOATING LABELS system.

---

[1] An extended version of this paper also includes the complete layout algorithm
(http://wwwisg.cs.uni-magdeburg.de/ hartmann/Papers/floating-labels.pdf).

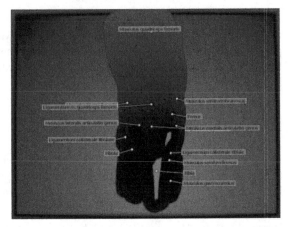

Fig. 3. A potential field for the tibia, a great bone located at the lower part of the knee joint. Red encodes attractive forces, and blue encodes repulsive forces. Black areas expose an equilibrium between attractive and repulsive forces.

The attractive force between a pictorial element and its associated labels is defined by:

$$U_{attr}(p) = \begin{cases} 0 & , p \in area(O) \\ c_1 \frac{\rho_O}{\eta} & , p \notin area(O) \end{cases}$$

For each object O which is projected on $area(O)$, ρ_O denotes the distance from p to the internal point $interia(O)$ and η the maximal distance from $interia(O)$ to the image boundary. This guarantees that the potential is within the interval $[0, 1]$. The constants c_i are some scaling factors. To prevent labels from overlapping the object's silhouette, a repulsive force U_{silh} is defined:

$$U_{silh}(p) = \begin{cases} c_2 & , \rho_{silh} \leq \rho_S \\ 0 & , \rho_{silh} > \rho_S \end{cases}$$

where ρ_{silh} denotes the minimal distance from p to object boundary and ρ_S is the silhouette influence factor. Another repulsive force should prevent labels floating outside the image boundary:

$$U_{wall}(p) = \begin{cases} c_3(1 - \frac{\rho_{wall}}{\rho_W}) & , \rho_{wall} \leq \rho_W \\ 0 & , \rho_{wall} > \rho_W \end{cases}$$

where ρ_{wall} denotes the minimal distance from p to the image boundary and ρ_W is the boundary influence factor. Finally, the repulsive force of non-associated objects is considered by:

$$U_{rep}(p) = \begin{cases} c_4 & , p \in area(O_i) \wedge O_i \neq O \\ 0 & , else \end{cases}$$

The potential field for a given object O is defined as the sum of the attractive and the maximal repulsive force:

$$U(p) = U_{attr}(p) + max(U_{wall}(p), U_{silh}(p), U_{rep}(p))$$

Figure 3 depicts the potential field for the tibia, which is partly occluded by the ligamentum patellae.

3.4   Initial Label Placement

After establishing the static potential field, label particles move from their start position until they reach minima within the potential field. Currently, we experiment with a set of initial label positions: (a) the corners of projection, (b) the internal point of the largest object segment *interia(O)*, and (c) a point on the preferred main axis.

Preferred Main Directions: Human illustrators prefer to connect label and anchor point with horizontal or vertical lines (Criterion 3). This observation guides the estimation of preferred label placements. Penalty values for four vectors starting from the anchor pointing to the main directions are computed. The penalty function considers:

- the number of non-reference objects which the connecting line crosses,
- the length of segments, where the connecting line crosses non-reference objects,
- the length of segments, where the connecting line crosses the reference object,
- the amount of available free length to place the label and its distance from the anchor point.

The penalty function aims at minimizing the number of non-referring pictorial elements crossed by connecting lines and the distance between the anchor point and the label. Figure 4 presents the preferred main axis to connect reference object and label.

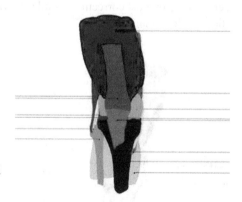

Fig. 4. Anchor points and preferred label directions.

3.5   Label Competition

While some of the label particles frequently reach identical local minima, there remain typically 3 different candidate positions. These candidates are measured according to a set of evaluation criteria: their *accumulated area potential* V_{pot}, their *visibility* V_{vis} (area not shared with other labels), the *length* V_{len} of the connecting line, and the minimal *angle* V_{angle} between the connecting line and either the horizontal or vertical axis. Due to space restrictions we will only present the first evaluation criterion:

$$V_{pot}(L) = \sum_{p \in \text{area}(L)} U(p), \text{L refers to the label under consideration}$$

In order to compare these different measures, they are normalized into a standard range [0,1]. Therefore, for each pictorial element and each criterion the best and worst values of the label candidate set are determined.[2] We found good results using a weighted sum of these measures, which enables us to consider global layout considerations. Figure 5-Left presents the label configuration after completing the first phase of the FLOATING LABELS algorithm.

3.6   Dynamic Force Field Calculation

The evaluation criteria aim at an even label distribution over the available space. Due to the ease of label replacement overlaps are not completely prohibited. A greedy re-adjustment algorithm is based on the assumption, that it is more easy to determine alternative appealing label positions for large objects than those for tiny objects.

Therefore, label overlaps are determined iteratively. One of these labels is selected and pinned on its current position. The selection criteria consider the visible area and the area of an axis-aligned bounding rectangle. Pinned label establishes repulsive forces over an extended label area, which is added to the static potential fields of all objects except it associated object. Then positions for the remaining unpinned labels are re-adjusted according to the corrected static potential fields (Force E). Figure 5-Right presents the final label configuration. The FLOATING LABELS system also enables the user to apply manual corrections, while the system computes a balanced label configuration for the remaining labels.[3]

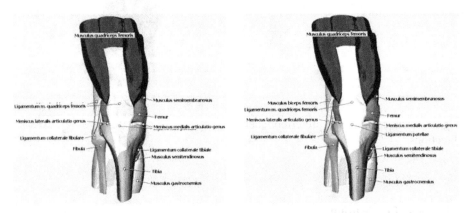

Fig. 5. Left: The initial label configuration for the knee joint. The model contains 19 different objects. 15 are visible from the current point of view, and 14 of them are big enough to place anchor points. **Right:** An improved label configuration. The greedy reposition algorithm was able to resolve both label overlappings.

---

[2] Note that these measures are either absolute (visibility) or relative (accumulated area potential, line length and angle).

[3] Not yet implemented.

3.7 Decoration

In this final step the meta-graphical objects (anchor points, connecting lines and labels) have to be integrated into an illustration in an aesthetic way. Therefore, we analyzed our corpus to extract appropriate render parameters for anchor points and connecting lines (e.g., shape, color). We found different rending styles:

Anchor Point Style: Some illustrators place them while others don't.

Connecting Line Style: Illustrators use either dashed or solid lines. Solid lines seem to segment the image into convex regions. In colored illustrations the choice of an appropriate line color is very difficult. Most illustrators prefer black, but they frequently use white when the connecting line overlays large dark regions. Frequently the connecting lines are absent for short distances between anchor point and label. Turns in the connecting line may also be used to prevent passing through dense, very detailed regions or to prevent label overlaps.

In order to guarantee the visibility in all regions, the current implementation uses solid white line with black shadows for both anchor points and connecting lines.

3.8 Software

The FLOATING LABELS algorithm is based on 2D projections of 3D geometric models from manually selected view points. Whenever hand-made illustrations of a similar object were available, we adjusted these view points of the 3D models to match these hand-made illustrations. Frequently, anatomic model are displayed from a set of different canonical viewing directions and thus several views of the same object are contained in our test set.

The 3D renderer is implemented in Open Inventor (Coin3D) and uses Qt to display the 2D image processing results. The basic algorithms are fully implemented, whereas the code and optimizations for user interactions have to be finished until the time of presentation. The runtime to compute the label layout for complicated views was up to 10 seconds on a modern PC.

4 Results

We tested our algorithm on more than 300 different geometric models taken from the ViewPoint library and Princeton 3D model search engine. Most of the geometric models do not separate individual objects. Even large 3D models with more than 100K vertices frequently did not segment them at all. For high-quality models the number of individual objects ranged between 10 and 25. The lack of highly segmented models was one of the main obstacles during testing.

Figure 6 presents some label configurations computed by the FLOATING LABELS system. Our algorithm fulfills Criteria 1–3 and 5. According to Criterion 4, crossings between connecting lines should be prevented as they are both distracting and misleading, the Criterion 6 refers to dynamic environments. Both criteria are not yet considered and subject to future work.

Within this limitation, we found the results quite promising. The label placement at local minima of potential field ensures an even label distribution. For illustrations with few labels even the label placement according to preferred main axis achieved good results. The consideration of repulsive force between labels in the second phase improves the label configuration on "hot spots", i.e., regions where many labels have to be arranged within small spatial areas. However, the most challenging example proves, that the static as well as the dynamic force field have to be fine-tuned and adjusted.

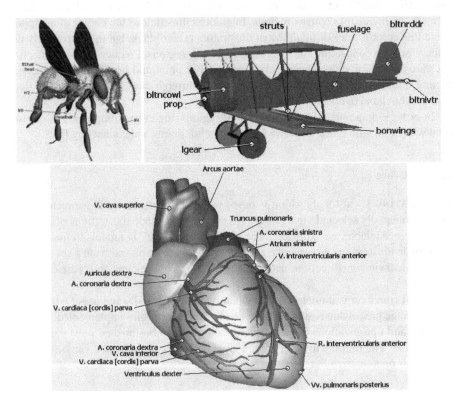

Fig. 6. Labels configurations automatically determined by the FLOATING LABELS system. For the heart model, the domain expert provided the denotation of geometric elements, whereas for the other models the internal descriptions are displayed in the label.

5   Improvement / Future Work

Human illustrators employ a variety of decoration styles (see Section 3.7). Hence, additional styles (e.g., labels without connecting lines, abbreviated label and legends) have to be integrated into the FLOATING LABELS system.

The current algorithm did not consider intersections of connecting lines. Based upon our observation how humans prevent unwanted intersections, we developed a strategy to resolve them. Whenever an intersection between two segments arises, the exchange of their label positions eliminates this intersection. Because labels do not overlap, this strategy can also be applied to labels of different sizes. A recursive application is able to resolve all intersections.

The main challenge is to integrate our force-field approach into an interactive 3D information system. While our first experiments use full-scaled projections, the reduction of quantization would speed-up the calculation considerably. Therefore, further experiments will analyze the accuracy-efficiency tradeoff. Moreover, hot spots can be observed after the initial label configuration, which might reduce the number of different potential fields required to balance them. Finally, alternative strategies to resolve conflicts, could be applied on hot spot areas (remove labels, shrink label text, alter height/width aspect of text boxes, legend creation . . .).

We plan to exploit shape approximations with bounding objects (object-oriented bounding boxes, sphere trees) to compute the forces and gradients analytically. This will reduce the amount of space required to store pixel-based approximations of potential fields and speed-up the calculation.

While the textual annotation or labels, as well as figure captions interrelate distant pictorial and textual segments, text balloon in comics embed almost all textual information within illustrations. Cartoon-style illustrations are especially attractive, as our algorithm can be also applied to determine appealing layouts for complex-shaped balloons. Special repulsive functions aim at avoiding visually important regions, like human faces and hands. Moreover, the algorithm is suitable to determine very complex layouts as required to design pictorial dictionaries. In all these application domains NPR shading techniques are most appropriate [18]. Hence, we will integrate our system into the OPENNPAR renderer [8].

6   Related Work

The automatic design of well balanced layouts is a central aspect within computer graphics, computational geometry, and cartography. A variety of different techniques have been applied to generate complex layouts automatically: constraints [11], simulated annealing [6], or genetic algorithms [12]. The authors have chosen the potential field method primarily as the observations presented in Section 1 could be transformed in a simple and elegant way to a variety of attractive and repulsive forces.

We created test set of several high-quality 3D models, and comparable hand-made illustrations, in order to extract human layout strategies and to evaluate our results. In order to compare different label layout techniques in terms of efficiency and visual balanced results, the authors plan to apply them on this test set.

The potential field method was successfully applied to plan paths for real objects like robots [10] as well as for virtual objects (e.g., camera planning in computer graphics). Several techniques were applied to prevent the object under control from getting stuck into local minima. To guide the planning, BECKHAUS [1] introduced navigation objects and dynamic potential fields. Our method has also to be compared with multi-agents path planning approaches in dynamic environments.

The appealing placement of labels is one of the central research subjects in cartography. Here, point-feature abstraction of labels have been frequently used (see [4]). EBNER [6] exploited force fields for the label number maximation problem for point features. Their approach aims at placing the maximal number of axis-aligned labels containing their reference points without any overlapping. In order to find global minima they combined a gradient-based and a simulated annealing approach.

PREIM [15] pioneered the interactive exploration of complex spatial configurations by visual and textual means. Textual annotation provides additional information about their co-referential geometric objects. Their content depends on the interaction context, which requires dynamic changes in size. Therefore, the spatial configuration of labels is adjusted by applying a 2D distortion technique. Moreover, PREIM and RAAB [14] employed mesh reduction to determine (multiple) anchor points for topographic complex geometric objects in 3D. However, the labels in these interactive information systems are either placed on special spatial area, placed manually or employ transparency to reduce the effect of occlusions.

BELL & FEINER [2] developed an algorithm to compute both covered and empty regions in dynamic environments, which was successfully applied for a dynamic label layout [3]. However, this algorithm is based on axis-aligned bounding boxes and does not yield best result for complex-shaped geometric object, whereas our algorithm works within the image space without such restrictions.

7 Conclusion

This paper introduces a label layout algorithm for complex-shaped geometric objects. It works on the image space without any approximation by bounding objects. Moreover, the label configuration is sensitive to global layout constraints, and can integrate user manipulations and automatic adaptations. Even though the FLOATING LABELS system is not yet integrated in an interactive 3D information system, our first experiments reveal a great potential of improvement and enhancement to speed-up calculations.

References

[1] S. Beckhaus, F. Ritter, and T. Strothotte. Guided Exploration with Dynamic Potential Fields: The CubicalPath System. *Computer Graphics Forum*, 20(4):201–210, Dec. 2001.

[2] B. Bell and S. Feiner. Dynamic Space Management for User Interfaces. In *Proc. of the 13th Annual Symposium on User Interface Software and Technology (UIST-00)*, pages 238–248. ACM Press, New York, 2000.

[3] B. Bell, S. Feiner, and T. Höllerer. Information at a Glance. *IEEE Computer Graphics and Applications*, 22(4):6–9, July/August 2002.

[4] J. Christensen, J. Marks, and S. Shieber. An Empirical Study of Algorithms for Point-Feature Label Placement. *ACM Transactions on Graphics*, 14:203–232, 1995.

[5] *The Oxford-Duden Pictorial English Dictionary*. Oxford University Press, 1995.

[6] D. Ebner, G. W. Klau, and R. Weiskircher. Force-Based Label Number Maximization. Technical Report TR-186-1-03-02, Institut für Computergraphik und Algorithmen, Technische Universität Wien, June 2003.

[7] H. Gray. *Anatomy of the Human Body*. Lea & Febiger, Philadelphia, 20th edition, 1918. http://www.bartleby.om/107/.

[8] N. Halper, T. Isenberg, F. Ritter, B. Freudenberg, O. Meruvia, S. Schlechtweg, and T. Strothotte. OpenNPAR: A System for Developing, Programming, and Designing Non-Photorealistic Animation and Rendering. In J. Rokne, R. Klein, and W. Wang, editors, *Proc. of Pacific Graphics 2003*, pages 424–428. IEEE Press, Los Alamitos, 2003.

[9] O. Khatib. Real-Time Obstacle Avoidance for Manipulators and Mobile Robots. *International Journal of Robotics Research*, 5(1):90–98, 1986.

[10] J.-C. Latombe. *Robot Motion Planning*. Kluwer Academic Publishers, Boston, 1991.

[11] S. Lok and S. Feiner. A Survey of Automated Layout Techniques for Information Presentations. In A. Butz, A. Krüger, P. Olivier, and M. Zhou, editors, *Proc. of the 1st International Symposium on Smart Graphics*, 2001.

[12] P. Olivier, N. Halper, J. Pickering, and P. Luna. Visual Composition as Optimisation. In *AISB Symposium on AI and Creativity in Entertainment and Visual Art*, pages 22–30, 1999.

[13] T. Pavlidis. A Thinning Algorithm for Discrete Binary Images. *Computer Graphics and Image Processing*, 13:142–157, 1980.

[14] B. Preim and A. Raab. Annotation topographisch komplizierter 3D-Modelle. In P. Lorenz and B. Preim, editors, *Simulation und Visualisierung '98*, pages 128–140. SCS-Society for Computer Simulation Int., Delft, 1998.

[15] B. Preim, A. Raab, and T. Strothotte. Coherent Zooming of Illustrations with 3D-Graphics and Text. In W. A. Davis, M. Mantei, and R. V. Klassen, editors, *Proc. of Graphics Interface '97*, pages 105–113. Canadian Information Processing Society, 1997.

[16] F. Ritter, H. Sonnet, K. Hartmann, and T. Strothotte. Illustrative Shadows: Integrating 3D and 2D Information Displays. In W. L. Johnson, E. André, and J. Domingue, editors, *Proc. of 2003 Int. Conf. on Intelligent User Interfaces (IUI'03)*, pages 166–173. ACM Press, New York, 2003.

[17] J. Sobotta, R. Putz, and R. Pabst, editors. *Sobotta: Atlas of Human Anatomy*. Lippincott Williams & Wilkins, Baltimure, 13. edition, 2001.

[18] T. Strothotte and S. Schlechtweg. *Non-Photorealistic Computer Graphics: Modeling, Rendering, and Animation*. Morgan Kaufman Publisher, Los Altos, 2002.

Calligraphic Editor for Textile and Tile Pattern Design System

José María Gomis, Francisco Albert, Manuel Contero, and Ferran Naya

DEGI, Universidad Politécnica de Valencia, Camino de Vera s/n,
46022 Valencia, Spain
{jmgomis, fraalgil, mcontero, fernasan}@degi.upv.es

Abstract. This paper presents a calligraphic editor for tile and textile design. This editor is part of an integrated system for graphic design, and includes also structural edition and retrieval tools to exploit design pattern databases. Drawing and some commands for geometrical transformations are specified by means of freehand strokes. Paper describes both user interface and its implementation details. A detailed design example is presented, where an ornamental motive, belonging to a pattern design has been generated by the gestural interface. Then it is integrated in a textile design using structural edition tools, based on the scientific theory of symmetry groups.

1 Sketching, Cultural Heritage, and Creativity in Graphic Design

The creative process is the sum of conscious and subconscious activities and is always associated with significant intellectual effort. In the conscious activities, the person involved in a creative process controls his/her mind, being capable of conducting the process of analysis and synthesis as well as of evaluating the given results. These activities are carried out within a context where the level of knowledge of the individual and the available technical resources can boost the results [1].

For the graphic designer, drawing is not only a means to communicate information concerning the product's fabrication and commercialisation, but it is also a means of exteriorising thoughts and ideas. As a consequence the skill to draw can mean a huge advantage in order to transmit the designer's intention at each stage. At the conceptual stage it is fundamental for the designer to have the ability to put his/her thoughts in order using the drawing (sketching) as a support [2].

However, nowadays, this drawing's role as a support tool of the creativity in the primary stages of graphic design is carried out aside from CAD/CAM environments. It is logical to believe that the integration of the conceptual drawing (sketch) in said environments would allow decreasing the time between the analysis-synthesis-evaluation stage and as consequence cut the time of the creative process cycles.

The graphic designer's creative process can also flourish by improving the capacity to visualise and to understanding his/her proposals within the system used for aided design. This understanding, on all different levels from the object to the structure, can speed up evaluation of the designs. In fact, the understanding and use of the

A. Butz et al. (Eds.): SG 2004, LNCS 3031, pp. 114-120, 2004.
© Springer-Verlag Berlin Heidelberg 2004

structural relationships in creative tasks were already educational objectives in Bauhaus [3]. They can be implemented and boosted within graphic design process by means of new techniques and specific methodologies.

On the other hand, in the design environment, the introduction of data in such a process is influenced by the social-cultural environment. In the case of graphic design where textile and tile industries are concerned, the Design Departments rely on different sources of graphic information which help designers in their creative tasks. The data sources consist of ancient designs, catalogues and magazines and in some cases even available specialized databases. Also in this case, integration of such sources in the graphic design platforms is both possible and desirable.

In our opinion, the promotion of the creativity and use of the artistic, craft and industrial historical heritage will be of great importance during the next few years in the textile and tile industries. Consequently, some of the most remarkable factors that will define graphic design platforms in the future are the following [4]:

1. Integration of the more conceptual stages of pattern design in integrated design and manufacturing systems. Integration involves two aspects: the use of specific and user-friendly peripheral devices and the development of interfaces which enables the use of the peripheral devices.
2. Development of advanced (structural) design tools for graphic design systems. The development of design tools, operating on all hierarchical levels of pattern design, will enhance the creative potential of designers who therefore will be able to adapt their methodological approaches to textile and tile design activities.
3. Creation and use of libraries at the different stages of the graphic design process. These libraries stored in databases would allow data consultation through content retrieval tools. Using the analogy of literary creation, these libraries will provide the designer with the existing formal vocabulary in addition to the lexicon he/she himself can add to his/her own creations

In this context, the authors of this work are developing an Information System for Graphic Design (ISGD). This system uses the theory of symmetry groups to structure the information obtained from design databases, helping to develop a graphic design methodology for the textile and tile industries [5]. In the following sections the edition capacity with objects and groups using a set of gestural tools specifically developed for this environment is explained. In section 5 we can see one edition example using gestural tools, where we have used also structural tools and transactions with the design databases.

2   Related Work

Nowadays, most of the commercial drawing and paint programs implement the WIMP interface paradigm. In this context some commercial tools have been developed for pattern design. For example, we can mention Terrazzo [7], available as a plug-in for Adobe Photoshop for raster edition, and SymmetryWorks [8], available as a plug-in for Adobe Illustrator for vectorial design. Introduction of Tablet-PCs at the end of 2002 have brought a new kind of drawing applications that integrates both shape and handwriting recognition such as Corel Grafigo.

Many research tools for automatic generation of symmetry patterns have been developed [9, 10, 11] mainly oriented to experiment with different algorithms for ornamental pattern creation. User interface has not been a critical issue for developing these tools. Commercial tools, as noted previously, are mainly concerned with supporting pattern parameter definition by means of the traditional WIMP elements. So, we think interesting to experiment with the new interaction paradigm proposed by the calligraphic approach, defining a basic gesture alphabet aimed at providing support for defining the main elements of patterns.

Widespread adoption of new hardware devices as digitizing LCD tablets and Tablets-PC is helping to adopt a more "user centric" user interface design to support ambiguity, creativity and informal communication. Some interesting examples of systems that use sketching and gesturing are: PerSketch [12] presents an image processing approach to perform covert recognition of visual structures as they emerge during a sketching session; Tahuti [13], is a dual-view sketch recognition environment for class diagrams in UML; ASSIST [14] enables sketching simple two dimensional mechanical systems in a natural fashion; Teddy [6] is oriented to free-form surface modelling.

3   User Interface

Calligraphic interface is activated using a special button added to the standard toolbox of Adobe Illustrator. Drawing and some commands for geometrical transformations are specified by freeform strokes drawn on the screen by a stylus. Strokes are composed by a set of coordinates (x,y) in an interval of pen-down and pen-up events.

3.1   Object Creation, Selection, Displacement, and Grouping

Objects are created by drawing a contour on the canvas. Open contours are automatically closed. Object selection is performed tapping on the object contour (drawing a small stroke) and dragging to the final position (in displacement mode strokes are not drawn). Feedback is provided to the user by highlighting object contour.

Surrounding some objects with a closed stroke is interpreted as a grouping action. After group centroid calculation, a set of lines are drawn linking the group centroid with each object centroid. Ungrouping action is performed drawing a scratch gesture on the line that links object with group centroid.

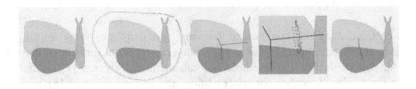

Fig. 1. Grouping and ungrouping example

3.2   Region Editing and Symmetry Operator

User can edit object contour by drawing a new object intersecting with it (if it is an open stroke, it is closed automatically). If new object is mostly in the outside then this is interpreted as an addition command. In the other case (shape mostly inside), a subtraction operation is performed.

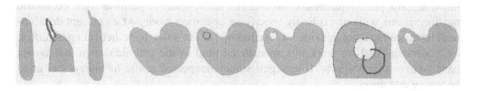

Fig. 2. Addition example on the left. Subtraction example on the right

Reflection symmetry gesture is represented by a line stroke. First and last points of the stroke define axis direction. (Last point also defines centre of symmetry if there are more than one axis). If we have selected some objects, and symmetry axis is external to them, these elements are replicated. If we have no selection, and axis goes across some objects, then new symmetrical objects are built. An optional hand drawn digit defines the symmetry order (number of axis).

Fig. 3. Reflection symmetry operator

Rotation symmetry gesture is defined by a circle. Its centre defines the rotation centre location. If we have selected some objects, and rotation centre is external to them, these elements are replicated. If we have no selection, and centre lays inside some object, then new object is built. A hand drawn digit defines number of fold repetitions.

Fig. 4. Rotation symmetry operator

4   Implementation

As noted previously, our application has been implemented as an Adobe Illustrator plug-in. This supposes that user can switch to the standard Illustrator tools in any moment, combining both WIMP and gestural interaction.

Our prototype plug-in has been designed in order to experiment with a modeless interface, similar in its objectives to the "Inferred-Mode Protocol" presented by Saund & Lank [16]. This means that user can draw, select or perform some geometric transformations without explicitly specify an operation mode. At its current development level we have not provided a "mediator" [17] to solve hypothetical ambiguities. We understand that we work in a specialized field inside graphic design that avoids many sources of ambiguity. If user gets some unexpected result, he always can undo the wrong operation.

In figure 8 we present a flowchart summarizing the gestural interface behaviour. It is organized around the events that user performs when he is making a stroke. The "mouse down", "mouse up" and "mouse move" events or the equivalent pen events if we are using a stylus for sketch input control the plug-in operation.

Taking into account the geometric characteristic of shapes found in textile and tile designs, we have chosen to implement a least squares fitting approach to interpolate piecewise cubic Bezier curves to define objects contours.

Object selection procedure is implemented by a "tapping" gesture. If user draws a small stroke on the object contour, it is interpreted as an object selection command. User can accumulate objects in the selection buffer, tapping again in other objects. Taping in free space means deselect all. Preliminary usability tests have shown this simple mechanism very effective.

Gesture recognition for tapping, symmetry, rotation and delete commands is performed using the following criteria: tapping is assumed if stroke length is under some predetermined threshold. Symmetry axis is detected if all points belonging to the stroke are located a distance less than a minimum value from the line define by the initial and end points of the stroke. Circle detection for rotation command is checked using the centre of the stroke bounding box as the theoretical centre of circle, and then testing that distance to that point along the stroke is similar. Scratch gesture is detected approximating the stroke by a polyline, and measuring angles between consecutive segments. A big number of small consecutive angles is interpreted as a scratch gesture. Hand written digits are recognized using the recognition services provided by Microsoft's Windows XP Tablet PC Edition.

The recognition of a symmetry or rotation gesture triggers a time-out event. This is used to perform digit recognition that will be interpreted as the order of the symmetry axis or rotation centre. Really this represents a mechanism to support a multistroke gesture, composed by a graphic sign and a digit.

Finally, it is important to note that we apply some perceptual rules to determine the behaviour of a stroke representing a closed loop. If it contains completely some objects it means a grouping operation. If it is completely inside of another object it performs a subtraction operation. Partial superposition with another object causes a subtract or addition operation if it is mostly inside or outside. Inclusion and superposition checking is performed using a standard raster colouring algorithm.

5   Results

Preliminary results obtained using the calligraphic editor have been very satisfactory. Users find intuitive and easy to use and learn the new edition tools. In figure 9 we present a design example that summarizes the main capabilities of our system. Above on the left we can see a pattern design constructed using the gestural edition tools described before. In the middle figure on left we can observe a textile image and some elements (Fundamental Parallelogram and groups of objects) obtained from its analysis available in the Design Pattern Database. On the right, one of the groups created with the gestural tool is replaced by a new group retrieved from the database. Finally, figure below show a structural edition applied to the previous design. On the left we can see the two templates (tiling and group) and the Minimum Region used to create the new Design.

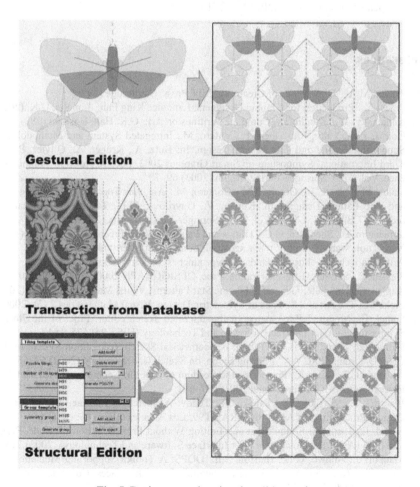

Fig. 5. Design example using the edition tool

6 Conclusions and Future Work

A calligraphic editor for a tile and textile design pattern module has been described. The module is part of an integrated system for graphic design, and includes also structural edition and retrieval tools to exploit design pattern databases. Gesture based editing is intended to support conceptual drawing in the system. Future work is oriented to extend the gestural interface to the whole design process allowing hierarchical edition and fundamental parallelogram and minimum region control.

Acknowledgments

This work has been supported by the Spanish Science and Technology Ministry and the European Union (Project DPI2001-2713).

References

1. Boden, M.A.: Dimensions of Creativity. MIT Press, Cambridge (1996)
2. Pipes, A.: Production for Graphic Designers. Laurence King Pub., London, U.K. (2001)
3. Kandinsky, W.: Kandinsky, Complete Writings on Art. G.K. Hall, Boston (1982)
4. Gomis, J.M., Valor, M., Albert, F.,Contero, M.: Intregated System and Methodology for Supporting Textile and Tile Pattern Design. In: Butz, A., Krüger, A., Olivier, P. (eds.): Third International Symposium on Smart Graphics 2003. Lecture Notes in Computer Science, Vol. 2733. Springer-Verlag, Berlin (2003) 69–78
5. Valor, M., Albert, F., Gomis, J.M., Contero, M.: Analysis Tool for Cataloguing Textile and Tile Pattern Designs. In: Kumar, V., Gavrilova, M.L., Tan, C.J.K., L'Ecuyer, P. (eds.): ICCSA 2003. LNCS, Vol. 2669. Springer-Verlag, Berlin (2003) 569–578
6. Grünbaum, B., Shephard, G.C.: Tilings and Patterns. W. H. Freeman, New York (1987)
7. Xaos Tools web site <http://www.xaostools.com/products/terrmain.html>
8. Artlandia web site <http://artlandia.com/products/symmetryworks/ >
9. Kaplan, C., Salesin, D.: Escherization. Proc. Of SIGGRAPH 2000 (2000) 499–510
10. Kaplan, C.: Computer Generated Islamic Star Patterns. Visual Mathematics 2 (3) (2000)
11. Field, M.: The Art and Science of Symmetric Design. Visual Mathematics 2 (3) (2000)
12. Saund, E., Moran, T.P.: A perceptually-supported sketch editor. Proc. of the 7th ACM Symposium on User Interface Software and Technology (UIST 94) 175–184
13. Hammond, T. and Davis, R.: Tahuti: A Geometrical Sketch Recognition System for UML Class Diagrams. 2002 AAAI Spring Symp. on Sketch Understanding (2002) 59–66
14. Alvarado C.J., Davis R.: Preserving the freedom of paper in a computer-based sketch tool. Proceedings of HCI International 2001, 687–691
15. Igarashi, T., Matsuoka, S., Tanaka, H.: Teddy: A Sketching Interface for 3D Freeform Design. Proceedings of ACM SIGGRAPH'99, Los Angeles (1999) 409–416
16. Saund, E., Lank, E.: Stylus Input and Editing Without Prior Selection of Mode, Proc. Of UIST '03 (ACM Symposium on User Interface Software and Technology) (2003) 213–216
17. Mankoff J., Abowd, G.D., Hudson, S.E.: OOPS: A Toolkit Supporting Mediation Techniques for Resolving Ambiguity in Recognition-Based Interfaces. Computers and Graphics 24(6) (2000) 819–834

Evaluation of User-Friendliness of a Compact Input Device with Simple Tactile Feedback

Itsuo Kumazawa

Imaging Science and Engineering Laboratory, Tokyo Institute of Technology,
Yokohama 226-8503, Japan
kumazawa@isl.titech.ac.jp

Abstract. Compact input devices are rather user-unfriendly because their narrow key pitch confuses finger pressure at a key touch pad. We have attempted to improve user-friendliness of such input devices by introducing a mechanism that enhances tactile feedback and creating an illusion of more distinguishable tactile space than the actual one. A trial model with such a mechanism is demonstrated and a GUI in association with haptic feedback of the device is effectively introduced.

1 Introduction

Various tactile and kinesthetic feedback mechanisms have been proposed. SP-IDAR [1], the pioneer of haptic interface study, generates kinesthetic feedback using threads, as suggested by its name. It generates forces of many degrees of freedom in 3D space. PHANToM [2], which applies kinesthetic feedback to a fingertip using a multi-joint mechanism, has achieved commercial success attributable to its ease of maintenance. Nevertheless, it allows only limited degrees of freedom of forces. These instruments are too large and consume too much electric power for use as a user interface with a small portable device. On the other hand, systems that can be miniaturized and which are advantageous to carry have been studied: optimal constitution of a pin display [3], development of a globe-shaped kinesthetic generation device [4], and an electric stimulation device that selectively stimulates skin sensory nerves [5]. Despite their advantages, they are rather burdensome for daily use. In view of such problems, the system proposed in this paper is implemented in a handy form like conventional cursor keys or a joystick, and is intended for small size, light weight, and low-power consumption. NaviPoint[6] is also developped with the same scope and adding a function to the familiar stick-based pointing device but not intending to use an active tactile feedback as it assumes a limitted use for information browsing. In contrast to these previous works, this paper presents a multi-purpose handy device with a mechanism that enhances tactile feedback. With this active tactile feedback, users would feel virtual keys that are easy to identify within the narrow area of operation. A trial model with such a mechanism is demonstrated and a GUI in association with the tactile feedback is effectively introduced especially while practicing controlling the devices. Although the device needs practice for

A. Butz et al. (Eds.): SG 2004, LNCS 3031, pp. 121–127, 2004.
© Springer-Verlag Berlin Heidelberg 2004

inexperienced users, we believe a smart GUI would guide such users and help their training.

2   Expansion of Tactile Space by Tactile Enhancement Mechanism

A magnifying glass enlarges a display screen so that a small character is enlarged and easy to read. This anticipates a means to enlarge a tactually sensed space: operating a device by touch-typing following tactile sense of the user allows a user to feel narrowly-aligned tiny buttons as widely-placed big buttons. This system improves the user-friendliness of an input device. If cost and size of such a device are ignored, a mechanism to expand tactile space in this way can be realized with the device shown in Fig. 1. The probe in Fig. 1 moves together with the fingertip; it measures the height of the object surface at the location of movement. Meanwhile, the actuator, moving along with the fingertip, moves the projection up and down based on the height measured by the probe. Thereby, it stimulates the tactile sense of the fingertip. For example, when the vertical and horizontal unevenness on the object surface are about several micrometers, the unevenness cannot be perceived even by direct fingertip contact. However, assuming that the fingertip travels by 1 mm in the device of Fig. 1, the probe is linked to travel by 1 μ m and the actuator displaces the projection up and down to magnify the vertical unevenness 1000 times. Thereby, a user has the illusion that the projection that moves up and down during movement of the fingertip is the unevenness of the imaginary surface. In this manner, a user can perceive fine unevenness on the object surface as tactually magnified. This technique to magnify sense in touching micro unevenness is applied for improvement in user-friendliness of a micromanipulation system. It may be inferred that expanding imaginary key pitch will improve user-friendliness if the device shown in Fig. 1 is implemented in a small input device. However, a larger input device is required because the travel range of a fingertip to press imaginary keys enlarges as the key pitch is expanded. The device in Fig. 1 enlarges the travel range of a fingertip and magnifies a tactile stimulus at the same time by manipulating both action and response of the feedback loop of the human kinesthetic system shown in Fig. 2. In order to produce a compact input device, it is crucial that tactile feedback be emphasized with small fingertip travel distance. That is, the unevenness of the surface touched by a fingertip changes abruptly with slight fingertip movement, so a button is perceived and distinguished clearly.

3   Virtual Keys Identifiable by Tactile Enhancement Mechanism

If correspondence with a real uneven surface is ignored in the device in Fig. 1, a large displacement of a projection in accordance with a slight travel of a fingertip can greatly change the feeling of unevenness that the fingertip perceives. Unless

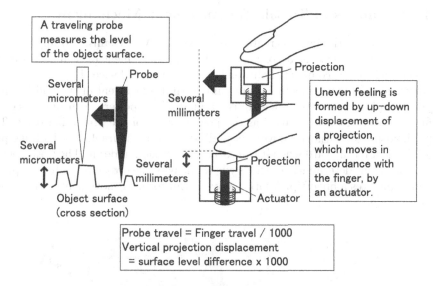

Fig. 1. Haptic feedback device to enlarge a tactually sensed space.

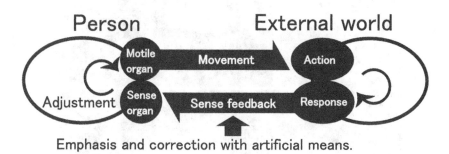

Fig. 2. Emphasis and correction of human and environment interaction by a tactile device.

a fingertip travels roughly, the feeling of unevenness does not change very much on a real uneven surface. So it is a strange experience in which a slight travel of a fingertip provides the feel of abrupt change of sense at the fingertip. This strangeness arises as a result of the inconsistency between an action and its tactile feedback. Our study aims to utilize this inconsistency for the purpose of creating a user-friendly input device and user interface. For example, if the tactile feedback to finger motion is emphasized, humans would be able to utilize this feedback to control a fingertip precisely based on such difference in this emphasized uneven feeling. Improvement of accuracy of motion may allow the input of diverse information without fingertip motion confusion, even on a narrow control panel.

4   Examples of Tactile Enhancement Mechanism

Figure 3 shows the device created in this study. A mechanism to apply tactile feedback emphasized in accordance with slight movement of a fingertip is implemented into a compact, lightweight, and low-cost device. Finger movement is transformed mechanically into up and down displacement of the ball-like projection in Fig. 3, and the fingertip is stimulated. No power is consumed because finger movement itself is used as the power source of the projection drive. The mechanism to transform movement is illustrated in Figure 4. The ball-like projection is lifted upward when it runs over a protrusion under it. The arrangement of protrusions determines positions where the ball-like projection is lifted upward and stimulates a fingertip. Another way of transforming movement is also shown in Figure 5.

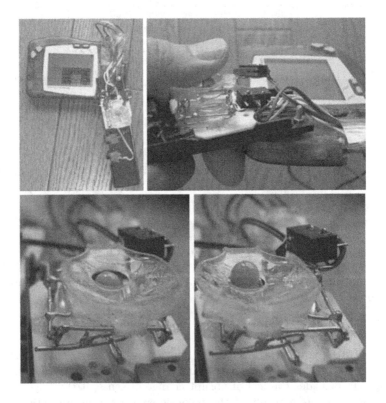

Fig. 3. Development of a PDA equipped with a tactile magnifier. This device is used to evaluate the effectiveness of emphasized tactile feedback on human and machine interaction. Up-down displacement of a ball-shaped projection helps the user to identify his or her finger position.

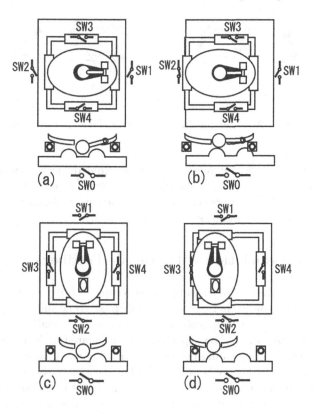

Fig. 4. A mechanism to transfer finger movement into up and down displacement of the ball-like projection.

5   Efficiency and Reliability of Input Operation

If four protrusions are introduced to the mechanism of Figure 4 and the ball-like projection is lifted up when the fingertip moves forward, backward, leftward and rightward, nine fingertip locations can be distinguished based on the feeling of unevenness created by the projection movement and this device allows input of nine kinds of different information. Comparing to the ordinary joystick or other pointing devices, this emphasized tactile feedback makes it easy and clear for a user to distinguish his or her fingertip position or movement while touch-typing. So the reliability and efficiency of data input operation are expected to increase. We examined this possibility through a simple task of inputting nine numeric characters. Around 25 seconds were required for 10 repeated inputs of a set of numbers from 1 to 9 in ascending order. The same work with a cellular phone takes 25 seconds when it was performed looking at the finger, while it takes 17 seconds with the numeric keypad of a PC. Although the input speed of the proposed device is equivalent to that of a cellular phone, this device allows input "in perfect touch-typing aided only by a sense of unevenness" in a small area

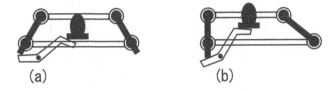

(a)   (b)

Fig. 5. Another mechanism to transfer the movement.

of about 2 cm^2. A large difference from other input devices, such as a joystick, is the feel of a projection that rises when a finger is moved. The present device improves user-friendliness because of this sensation; it allows a user operation along discriminating information to be input clearly.

6   GUI in Association with Tactile Feedback

Although the effectiveness of the simple and compact haptic feedback mechanism on input of nine numeric characters was confirmed, some suitable graphical user interface for the input device needs to be developed especially for training purposes. Although users would be expected to manipulate the device only by tactile clues after practice, they would need a proper graphical guidance while mastering the operation. In Figure 6 and 7, the lattice with 9 square areas suggests the nine different fingertip locations distinguished by the up-down movement of the projection and the small circle suggests that the projection moves up and stimulates the fingertip at the location. Each arrow in Figure 6 suggests a fingertip movement and a letter associated with each arrow is inputted when the corresponding finger action is performed. What is different from other gesture-based interfaces using ordinary pointing devices is the active haptic feedback which helps the user to perform the action precisely and with high reliability. Without tactile clues we tends to mislead our fingers particularly when quick action is required. In Figure 7 the lattice with 9 square areas is used as an icon for each item. When the finger action implied by the icon is performed, the corresponding item is chosen. These two ways of giving graphical clues are still not sufficient and we should explore more suitable graphical user interface. Just like the pointing-based graphical user interface effectively used with the mouse, there should be a way of introducing graphics effectively for the active-haptic-feedback devices.

References

1. Sato, M., Hirata, Y. and Kawarada, H.: SPIDAR: A Space Interface Device. IEICE Transactions **J74-D-II** (1991) no. 7, 887–894
2. Massie, T.M. and Salisbury, J.K.: The PHANToM haptic interface: A device for probing virtual objects. Proc. ASME Dynamic Systems and Control Division **55** (1994) 295–301

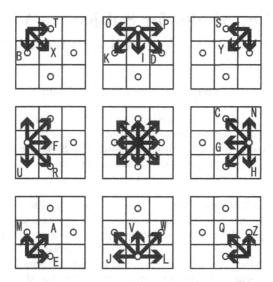

Fig. 6. Graphical guides for character input. A letter associated with an arrow inputs when the finger movement suggested by the arrow is performed with the guide of haptic feedback implied by the small circle.

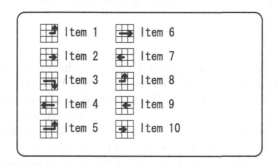

Fig. 7. Icons suggesting finger movement and tactile feedback.

3. Shimojo, M., Shinohara, M. and Fukui, Y.: Shape recognition performance and density of presented pins for 3D tactile display. IEICE Transactions **J80-D-II** (1997) no. 5, 1202–1208
4. Fujita, K.: Development and evaluation of glove-shaped virtual object hardness presentation device. IEICE Transactions **J81-D-II** (1998) no. 10, 2394–2400
5. Kajimoto, H., Kawakami, N., Maeda, T., and Tachi, S.: Electric tactile display which selectively stimulates skin sensory nerves. IEICE Transactions **J84-D-II** (2001) no. 1, 120–128
6. Kawachiya, K., and Ishikawa, H.: NaviPoint: An Input Device for Mobile Information Browsing. Proc. ACM CHI '98 Conference (1998), 1–8

Petri Net Model for Subjective Views in Collaborative Virtual Environments

Jianghui Ying and Denis Gračanin

Virginia Tech
Department of Computer Science
7054 Haycock Road, Falls Church VA 22043, USA
jying@vt.edu, gracanin@vt.edu

Abstract. Collaborative Virtual Environments (CVEs) use a shared virtual world for interactions and collaboration among users. Most current CVEs provide a highly objective virtual environment. Some degree of subjectivity is necessary to support collaboration in virtual environments. Subjective views can provide benefits to users but they can also pose problems. The current generation of event-based software, languages, methods, and tools cannot serve virtual reality (VR) interfaces well. We propose a new approach to describe and implement multi-user VR interfaces that support subjective views. Petri net theory is the formalism selected to model a virtual world and to support subjectivity while providing consistent collaboration and interactions among users.

1 Introduction

Collaborative Virtual Environments (CVEs) use a shared virtual world to support interactions and collaboration among users. CVEs provide a shared 3D space for users and many types of 3D artifacts. Most of the current CVEs provide a highly objective virtual environment. That is, each user is presented with the same virtual world in the same way, albeit from different viewpoints. This is partly due to the fact that multi-user Virtual Reality (VR) systems have evolved from single-user VR systems that have been extended to support many users.

The development trend for the VR systems is similar to the way that groupware system evolved from 2D single-user systems that simply replicated the single-user interface to multiple users. This simple replication of the system's interface secured a founding abstraction for multi-user interfaces: What You See Is What I See (WYSIWIS). WYSIWIS can create the sense of teamwork so it is critical for collaboration, however, some research indicates that strict objectivity is too inflexible [1]. Just as strict objectivity proved too constraining in groupware systems, a degree of subjectivity is necessary to support collaboration in Virtual Environments (VEs). Snowdon introduced the term "subjective views" for the concept of multiple perspectives in VEs [2]. The subjectivity is defined as the ability to add viewer dependent features to a system (where a viewer maybe a "real" user or a software agent). The information presented to a viewer may depend on the viewer. A subjective VE can provide users ability to control the presentation style to best suit their working needs.

A. Butz et al. (Eds.): SG 2004, LNCS 3031, pp. 128–134, 2004.
© Springer-Verlag Berlin Heidelberg 2004

2   Motivation and Related Work

In current CVEs, subjectivity does make a limited appearance. For example, each user is given an independent virtual body and has a unique viewpoint in the virtual world. There are many potential uses of subjective views [2]. In addition to providing customization capability to CVEs, subjective views can also be used to support CVEs that are accessible from different devices and hardware/software configurations. However if subjective views diverge beyond a certain point, meaningful collaboration will become difficult or even impossible. Activities of users with totally different views may cause some confusion, especially when users attempt to communicate what they see to each other.

The research in shared 2D user interface systems is used as a starting point to model subjective views in CVEs. Smith and Mariani describe the SOLVEN model [3] for subjective views. The core feature is an access matrix that defines the representation of individual objects for individual users. The object's representation is determined by two independent factors: appearance and modifier.

3   Petri Net Based User Interface Modelling

Formal methods have been applied for the development of user interfaces with two aims: to abstract from the details of users, software, and their interaction as a basis for reasoning and analysis, and to ensure correct implementation of software requirements. As user interfaces become more complex, it becomes more important to communicate among interface designer, developers, users and customers the look and functionality of a proposed interface. A formal specification of user interface provides a number of advantages, such as early use in the design process, better prediction of usability aspects, precision for design and communication, and enabling automatic generation of user interfaces.

Petri net (PN) [4] is a directed graph consisting of two types of nodes: places and transitions. A place and a transition are connected by an arc either from a place to a transition or vice versa. In a graphical representation, places are drawn as circles and transitions as boxes. Each place has an assigned marking (state) with k tokens, in which k is a nonnegative integer. The graph has an initial state called the initial marking, M.

We select PN instead of other formal methods to model user interface, because the input/output of VR interface always occur concurrently. PN is a behavior-based formal method, which define systems in terms of possible sequences of states and can model concurrent activities. There are some works applying PNs to user interface design, such as OSU [5] but all previous work focused on 2D user interface design.

Most of tasks performed within a VE are application-specific so it is difficult to model all of them. However, there are some basic interactions that most VE interactions are composed of. The majority of VE interactions fall into three task categories: navigation, selection/manipulation, and system control [6]. Navigation is the most prevalent user action in most virtual environments. Manipulation involves changing properties of virtual objects such as position, orientation, scale, shape, etc. Manipulation always implies selection, but selection may be a stand-alone task. System control covers other commands that the user gives to accomplish work within the application, such as save the current scene, etc.

If PNs can be used to model these basic interactions, other complex tasks could also be modelled. The space in a VE is constructed using a number of virtual objects. The state of the VE is determined by the state of each object. A PN model of the VE captures the state change of each object and describes the whole VE's state. Within a PN, the places represent the state of the objects. The transitions refer to how users interact with the objects.

Selection and manipulation usually involve touching an object, and then changing its properties like position, orientation, scale, etc. For example, a user controls by mouse a virtual hand to move a cup in a VE. The cup may be in three states: *free*, *available*, and *active*. When the user moves the virtual hand to touch the *free* cup, the cup is *selected* and becomes *active*. The user could then move the virtual hand to change position of the cup.

This example can be modelled using a corresponding PN, as shown in Figure 1. The three states of the cup are represented with three places. The state migration is triggered by user actions, which are represented by transitions. When a user interacts with an interface, the user changes the state of the interface and also observes the result of the state change. When multiple users collaborate in a VE, it is required that the collaborating users keep a consistent understanding of the shared interface. This requires a separation between the collaborative interface specific information from the underlying application functionality (semantics). For example, the "focus in" label can be replaced by a "select" or "click right mouse button." The PN remains the same.

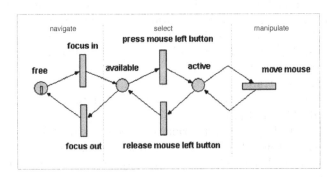

Fig. 1. Petri net model example

The application functionality (semantics) must be the same or nearly the same for all users in the CVE. It is the only way to maintain effective collaboration. However, what an individual user can do may be very different. In other words, at the semantic level, users must observe the same things but how are those things presented is another question.

4   Automatic Petri Net Generation

Currently there are many 3D file formats that describe a VE for the purpose of visualization (VRML, X3D, 3DML, Cult3D, XGL, etc.) [7]. These file formats describe geometric models and their corresponding relationships and properties as they are defined within that file. These file formats serve as the starting point for automatic PN generation. Regardless of the format used, it is necessary to automatically build a PN based on the VE description. Since PN mainly describes how user interaction changes the state of the VE, the first step is to extract information about user interaction and how the interaction changes the properties of objects. The extracted information is then put into an Interaction Specification List (ISL) file, which is an intermediate XML-based file to be translated to another XML-based interchange format for PN, Petri Net Markup Language (PNML) [8]. The PNML file is then used in a PN based tool. Virtual Reality Modelling Language (VRML) is used as a test case to show how to extract necessary information from a VE and translate into a PN model.

4.1   User Interaction Extraction

Besides 3D content description, 3D file formats typically have an inherent event model. An event has a life cycle that begins with the action or condition that initiates the event and ends with the final response. The life cycle of a typical event consists of the following steps: user action or condition occurs, event instance is created, event fires, event propagates, and event related behavior is triggered.

There are two types of event providers. One type includes external sources, like mouse, glove, keyboard, etc. Normally, a user fires an event by manipulating external input devices. The other type of events include internal sources, like timers or a user defined functions or routines, which can generate any type of events. Normally user interactions are based on external sources, however, the internal sources may be also involved when an event needs to propagate to other nodes in the scene graph. The event model provides the necessary information about user interactions. Although different file formats use different way to propagate events, it is sufficient to know the result of each action.

4.2   Interaction Specification List

The proposed approach is to have a common format to describe the user interaction information extracted from different 3D file formats to be able to automatically interpret semantic information. This information is used to create a PN. XML and related technologies offer a flexible implementation platform. An XML-derived language, Interaction Markup Language (IML), is used to describe how user interactions take place in a virtual world. The interaction specification list treats everything in the virtual world as and object, including virtual 3D objects representing users, viewpoints, virtual controls, etc. Each object has several states representing different stages based on event stimulation. The state migration is triggered by user interactions (directly or indirectly).

Figure 2 shows an example of how to present potential interactions from a VRML file (Figure 2a) in an IML file (Figure 2b). The virtual world consists of a single cube that can rotate (click). In the IML file, all possible states for the cube (*GreenBox*) are listed. That includes *still*, *ready*, and *rotate*. Three user interactions are possible: "focus in," "click," and "focus out."

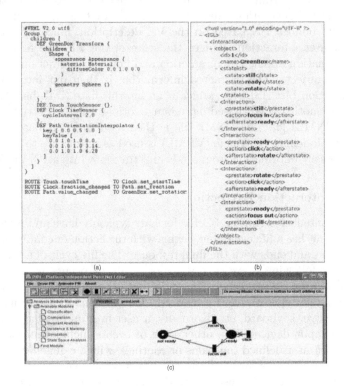

Fig. 2. VRML, IML and PN examples

The IML document includes one or more objects. Each object is composed of property elements (id, name, etc.), one statelist, and zero or one interaction element. Each interaction element has *prestate* tag to describe the state accepts the action as well as *afterstate* tag for the resulting state. User's interaction may change the object's properties as well as send events to other objects to trigger some other events/interactions. The *AffectedProperty* element describes which property will be changed according to user interaction. The *EventIn* element defines all messages sent by other interactions user makes on this object or other objects. When the object receives a message, some properties could be changed. On the other side, the *EventOut* element defines all messages that this interaction may send to other interactions in this object or other objects. Sender and receiver in *EventIn* or *EventOut* describe the message with *object_id*, *interaction_id*, and *result/msg*.

The IML document content must be presented in a format that a PN modelling tool can understand. The generic interchange format (PNML), defines typical features of all PNs and allows for future extensions [8].

5   Translation

We have developed a prototype translator from VRML to PNML. The translator uses an open source VRML parser pw to parse a VRML file and get all components from the virtual world. Based on the analysis of each VRML node type, there is a set of nodes that have implicit user interaction information. Normally such nodes have no visible geometry, but they influence other visible nodes in a specific way when user manipulate the visible nodes. For example, an *Anchor* node that is in the same group with a *Box* node implies several user interaction steps on the *Box*: "focus in" on *Box*, "press mouse button," etc.

Specific XML tags describe such interaction steps. When the parser finds such nodes in a VRML file, the corresponding tags are generated in the destination IML file. Since both IML and PNML are XML-derived languages, an XSLT stylesheet is used for transformation. Figure 2c shows the resulting PN.

The main challenge is translating from VRML to IML. When the parser parse a VRML file, it can get all objects that will be influenced by a specific user action by analyzing the hierarchy structure and event routing in VRML. In IML, these objects have corresponding XML elements describing each interaction step. One could only use an abstract state to represent the result of the user interaction. For example, a cube is rotating after clicking. One could only use the state "rotate" to describe the result, but how it rotates is difficult to specify (speed, orientation, etc.). The change of these properties is normally defined with *Interpolator* or *Script* nodes. If defined in an *Interpolator* node, it is possible to get information how the properties are changed since the definition of the *Interpolator* node is known. However, if the property change is defined in a *Script* node, the result is undetermined because the *Script* node can change other nodes' properties by sending an *EventOut* or directly changing property values in *Script* node functions.

6   Subjectivity

When user interacts with the VE user interface, the state change will be reflected in the PN. A user's view is derived from a common interface that is constructed from a collection of all shared virtual objects. Managing each user interface is achieved through the manipulation of access to this common VE interface. One could construct the common PN to describe the whole picture of the VE interface. The goal is to make a consistent understanding of the VE among users. Each user has a customized user interface and the corresponding PN. The corresponding PN describes all the interactions available to the user. Those interactions include controlling the VE or changing the view. If needed, there may be a group level PN that integrates individual user interfaces and available interactions. The common PN captures all available interactions. The changes in user interfaces create changes in the common PN.

The example shown in Figure 1 illustrates the PN model that can be generated from many different subjective views. Differences in nature of interactions and presentation of objects do not affect the semantics of interactions and tasks performed. As a consequence, we can establish a common framework for all subjective views. User's interactions can be modelled and evaluated using PN properties thus providing a way for quantitative comparisons. The mapping between the virtual world and the PN is many-to-one. Therefore, one PN can control several subjective views.

7   Conclusion

PN theory is a formalism selected to model subjective views and interactions in CVEs. We have developed a prototype translator for automatic conversion from a virtual world to the corresponding PN. Different subjective views of the same virtual world can be represented with the same underlying PN thus providing a common framework necessary for collaboration. The current work is focusing on completing the translation process. That requires more detailed description about the virtual scene besides the interaction and event flow information. This approach will help improve our understanding and modeling of user interactions in CVEs.

References

1. Stefik, M., Bobrow, D.G., Foster, G., Lanning, S., Tatar, D.: WYSIWIS revised: Early experiences with multiuser interfaces. ACM Transactions on Information Systems (TOIS) **5** (1987) 147–167
2. Snowdon, D., Greenhalgh, C., Benford, S.: What you see is not what i see: Subjectivity in virtual environments. In: Framework for Immersive Virtual Environments (FIVE'95), QMW University of London, UK (1995)
3. Smith, G., Mariani, J.: Using subjective views to enhance 3D applications. In: Proceedings of the ACM symposium on Virtual reality software and technology, ACM Press (1997) 139–146
4. Peterson, J.L.: Petri Net Theory and the Modeling of Systems. Prentice-Hall, Englewood Cliffs, New Jersey 07632 (1981)
5. Keh, H.C., Lewis, T.G.: Direct-manipulation user interface modeling with high-level Petri nets. In: Proceedings of the 19th annual conference on Computer Science, ACM Press (1991) 487–495
6. Bowman, D.A., Kruijff, E., LaViola, Jr., J.J., Poupyrev, I.: An introduction to 3-D user interface design. Presence **10** (2001) 96–108
7. Walsh, A.E., Borges-Sévenier, M.: Core Web3D. Prentice Hall PTR, Upper Saddle River, NJ 07458 (2001)
8. Billington, J., Christensen, S., van Hee, K., Kindler, E., Kummer, O., Petrucci, L., Post, R., Stehno, C. and Weber, M. : The Petri Net Markup Language: Concepts, technology and tools. In: Proceedings of the 24th International Conference on Application and Theory of Petri Nets (ICATPN'2003), Eindhoven, The Netherlands, June 2003, volume 2679 of LNCS. Springer (2003) 483–505

Smart Garden: Plant Mail and Chat Environments

Daniel Rivera, Isaac Rudomin, and Marissa Diaz

ITESM-CEM, Atizapan Mexico
rudomin@itesm.mx,
http://rudomin.cem.itesm.mx

Abstract. We describe a series of applications that involve interfaces that allow a certain amount of "communication" with other living beings, in particular, plants. These interfaces allow the user to have contact with plants in ways which provide a better understanding of their "feelings" based on changes (humidity, chemistry) in the soil where the plant is "planted". We also explore the effects of the different kinds of interaction in changing the perception of people about other virtual and live entities.

1   Introduction

When a user interacts with a computer generated (virtual) or a computer enhanced world by using an interface, the user is in reality using metaphors. This allows him/her to correctly "connect" the actions carried out in the real world with what must happen in the application. Most work in this area has focused in the visual aspect of the interface, but other important aspects have been somewhat neglected. Tangible interfaces have been shown to make the user feel more connected to the virtual world [1] by using real world objects as interfaces.

The use of such interfaces is a powerful way of creating a strong impression on the user and making him/her believe that he/she is really interacting with the virtual world. But what are the best ways in which we can induce the user to suspend disbelief? Which tools have more impact?

We developed a series of applications that explore different aspects of what we call Virtual Reference, that are in fact an elaboration of a very simple idea: a natural environment that includes a real (natural) plant is connected to sensing devices. In these applications a user suspends disbelief and actually thinks that he/she is communicating with the plant(s). These applications use the computer as an enabling technology, but are not "computer graphics" in the traditional sense of using the screen to display the virtual world, yet they are still visual in the even more traditional sense of sculpture and installation. We call it "real virtuality" for lack of a better term[2]. Here there is no screen with a graphical representation of the virtual world, so the user may have only a reference that doesnt really exist but yet relates the application with a real object. It is important to point out that this lack of pixel graphics is due to artistic rather than technical reasons. Even when the user doesnt have direct contact with these

A. Butz et al. (Eds.): SG 2004, LNCS 3031, pp. 135–139, 2004.
© Springer-Verlag Berlin Heidelberg 2004

objects and he/she sees or imagines how the real object affects the virtual world and realizing how the action is performed, he/she still manages to construct a more direct metaphor.

In the following sections we describe these applications in detail, including the hardware developed specifically for this purpose. We discuss user reaction to these applications. Finally we discuss the lessons learned and the implications on interface design.

2   Plant with Humidity Sensor

A real plant is used as a virtual reference to the action of messaging for help. Here we do not use a computer. A simple humidity sensor is attached to the plant (actually the soil it is planted on) and when it is determined by the sensor that the humidity is low, and therefore the plant needs to be watered, a LED lights up (Figure 1(a)).

Fig. 1. Plant with sensor, (a)without computer interface (b) with computer interface, (c) with webcam

This sensing device simply closes a current loop using the humidity on the plant's soil, so when the water is missing the loop is broken and so the led turns on. This was exhibited in March 2003 at the International Festival of the Historic Center, X-Teresa Arte Actual, Mexico.

3   Email Plant

In this case the plant is used as a virtual reference to the action of sending a mail. A simple humidity sensor is attached to the plant and when it is determined by the software that the humidity is low, and therefore the plant needs to be watered, it sends an e-mail to the user or list of users. Figures 1(b)and 1(c) show the plant connected to a PC that sends the e-mails contained in the list. As shown above, the interface evolved because the plant required more power to communicate the current status to the remote user.

Technically, the interface of this plant consists of a humidity sensor that goes from the pot to a circuit that transforms the analog signal into discrete values and sends them to a PC by serial port. From there, a java application sends e-mails from a list of users and attaches a text file describing the status of the plant. Different plants require special humidity, minerals and other different factors such as PH levels, so more complex sensors could be used and the status of these variables could be stored in the micro controllers memory so the user could change the application specially for his/her plant. However, this application was developed specifically for the context of an art exhibit and thus the effects and metaphors could be achieved even with the simplest of sensors.

The audience/user introduces his/her e-mail address into the PC and adds it to the mailing list, so the plant can send messages to every address on it. The system sends one or several messages remarking that water is depleting. From this possibility, the specter of utility of the application grows, yet it widens and reaches the regions bounded by conceptual art.

We explored this with different shows in galleries (Mexico and Colombia), which we will detail later, but in general, we could see the following reaction from spectators: The daily interactions of most users with e-mail services made them take it for granted that a computer screen is used to send the e-mails; The love and care for and from the plant surpassed the barriers that that computers still generate in some users. The application drew a wide sector of people who normally withdraws from scientific and technological developments. We have speculated that the reason for this is that the computer can be ignored if the object is not displayed in the screen, in other words, there is no overload or abuse of virtual images, i.e. no pixels are perceived.

With this simple application we wanted to make the user think that there was communication with the plant and thus the user has the power to interact with another biological entity. Despite of the fact that the user knows that this kind of direct interaction is not possible, he/she establishes the necessary metaphor making him/her create stronger emotional bonds with the plant.

The virtual connection between the real (tangible) world and the virtual one must establish in the user's mind an idea of the relationship between the real objects, their function in the virtual word, and how his/her actions affects them [3]. This is true particularly when the goal is to represent an object of the virtual world with a specific object or allusion in the real world and, in the case of the mixture of nature, with virtual responses in an emulated world some kind of affective reference is needed. This affective reference is the link that the user gives to the real tangible media; it is the status that relates the user to other things in his/her life. One example of this affective reference is the idea that a plant could be sad, happy or angry by interpreting the status of the soil on which it is potted.

The bond or psychological link between the user and the virtual ambient is such that these interfaces can also resort to natural elements such as plants, that normally mean something to their owner, from only part of the decoration to truly beloved beings, they are important in the life of the user and people relates them to their own feelings and mood changes. This can be used as reinforcing element for interaction [4]. This application has been shown with variations at:

- September 2003 "Email Plant", Galeria Myto, Mexico
- November 2003-2004 "Email Plant 2" Valenzuela & Klenner Galeria, Bogota Colombia
- December 2003-2004 "Email Plant 3" Casa Frissac, Mexico

The variations were in the way the art was installed. Due to the fact that the show in Colombia had certain constraints, it was decided to show the application through a webpage with a webcam, and have the plant physically in Mexico City. This added an extra element of virtuality. In all cases, however, we received informal feedback from the attendees, and we could see that people were really surprised with the application. When pertinent, people immediately requested us to use their e-mail addresses. They were eager to receive e-mail from a plant, although they knew that the mail was not "really" from the plant. The users seemed to react to the virtual affection bond and cared for the status of the plant. More sophisticated viewers that had knowledge of conceptual art reacted intellectually, but everybody reacted by becoming emotionally attached to the plant.

4   Plant Chat

This section describes work in progress that is derived from the previous application.

Traditionally we have known that natural "messages", such as the change of color of a plant, for example, mean that it is dry or something else is wrong. Today we know that there are many other phenomena that stress plants. Plants communicate with each other trough chemical means. Salicylic acid, for example, can transmit to a neighboring plant the message that all is well.

In this sense, the semantics of data has become a primary objective in the understanding of scientific and technological results, giving way to the universe of metaphors, the recurring language of arts.

Smart Garden is an interface that inserted in this context will explore the relationship of plants amongst themselves, as well as between humans and plants. It will be a versatile installation that can be mounted in a garden, or indoors, but always with a mirror in the net, with mobile computing and telephony as components.

In this case we will sense not only humidity but also acidity (PH) in the plants and by doing this it in fact will intercept, decode, transmit (through internet) and reinterpret messages between plants (by applying the detected substances remotely); the system can be thus be considered as an "internet chat" between plants, in their own chemical language. The system will also "translate" these messages to humans, to a public that is physically present or remote. All this takes time in "plant time", which can be slow, so the system also needs to sense the proximity of humans to complete the esthetic act.

The public will follow the conversation of the plants as well as his/her own influence on them via a mobile phone or through a WiFi capable PDA, that will also allow the user to enter his/her e-mail address so that the user can follow the development of the conversation after he/she leaves the exhibit.

In summary, the public will be confronted with the augmented world of plants, in the net, but emphasizing physical presence in the exhibition place so that the piece works in its totality.

The technical work is very advanced and preliminary testing has been conducted. However, we must still install and test the complete application to be able to determine whether the reaction of users will be as interesting as it was for the previous pieces.

5   Conclusions

In the testing trials we have performed so far in several venues and with different installations, suspension of disbelief is achieved through the formation of metaphors, that allows the user to correctly "connect" the actions carried out in the real world with what must happen in the application. Applications that use some aspects of this sense are a powerful way of creating an illusionary link between what the user is seeing and interpreting, different interaction techniques and tricks must be developed for each kind of virtual environments. This is so because using always the already standard interfaces is environments causing a dangerous homogenization in a creative field. This is not good for visual artists and virtual reality specialists that want to create reactions, cause emotional responses and suspend disbelief.

References

1. Ishii, H.: Tangible Interfaces. In Proceedings of SIGGRAPH 1999, ACM Press / ACM SIGGRAPH, Annual Conference Series, pp 127.
2. Diaz, M. and Rudomin, I.: Object, function, action for tangible interface design. Accepted for publication in Proceedings Graphite 2004, ACM Press
3. Ogden, P. Human computer interaction in complex process control: developing structured mental models that allow operators to perform effectively. People in Control. IEE Conf. No. 481 . p 120 -125.
4. Ishii, H. Tangible bits: Towards Seamless interfaces between People, Bits and Atoms. In Proceedings of CHI97 ACM march 1997.

Automatic Collage Using Texture Synthesis

Stephen Ingram[1] and Pravin Bhat[2]

[1] Georgia Institute of Technology
Atlanta, GA USA
kronski@cc.gatech.edu
[2] Microsoft Corporation
Redmond, WA USA
prbhat@microsoft.com

Abstract. We present an application of texture synthesis in creating collages. We use the texture synthesis method proposed by Ashikhmin [1] to selectively copy patches of the source image onto the image to be stylized, creating an automatic collage. The underlying algorithm is fast and allows the user to iteratively improve the quality of the resulting image. We show the use of this algorithm in capturing various kinds of artistic qualities ranging from styles of famous painters to non photorealistic rendering.

1 Introduction

With computer science maturing as a discipline we have seen it take bold steps into domains previously believed to be a part of the exclusive human hegemony, beyond the reach of beast or machine. There was once a time when one's prowess in the game of Chess was considered to be a measure of general intelligence. Today, however, Chess has been reduced to a simple search problem. Arguably, the most coveted of these domains is the application of machines in learning and applying this learning to diverse paradigms. Known as creative thinking, some might argue that it will never be artificially implemented. Yet computer graphics in union with computer vision and machine learning has given rise to the new paradigm of *Smart Graphics*; possibly a stepping stone towards *Sentient Graphics*. Smart Graphics has been creatively used in applications ranging from rotoscoping to non-photorealistic rendering.

We are concerned with the problem of implementing the artistic technique known as collage. Collage is a cannibalistic art form, where a piece of art is deconstructed into its symbolic elements. These elements are then rearranged to create a new image. We allow the user to define what this new image should look like by specifying a target image which is used to determine the placement of symbolic elements obtained from a source image. The general solution to this problem is unknown, as the definition of what exactly constitutes to be a symbolic element in a given image is subjective in nature. Therefore, we narrow the scope of this problem to the genre of collages created using images that draw their distinctive style from constituent textures. In this case, the symbolic elements of an image are simply defined to be the textures the artist used to create the image. To create such a collage one would have to use the

A. Butz et al. (Eds.): SG 2004, LNCS 3031, pp. 140-145, 2004.
© Springer-Verlag Berlin Heidelberg 2004

source image as a palette of textures that would be selectively sampled to build a stylized version of the target image. This problem can be easily solved using the texture synthesis algorithm proposed by Ashikhmin to synthesize natural textures [1], which we extend in certain modest ways. Our primary contribution is not the modifications to the texture-synthesis algorithm, but its application in the domain of automatic collage.

We begin by providing a brief overview of related work in Section 2. In Section 3 we describe in detail the Ashikhmin texture synthesis algorithm. Section 4 presents our results and we conclude by discussing the limitations of our approach.

2 Related Work

Texture Synthesis. The use of texture synthesis and analysis to capture artistic styles isn't new. Texture synthesis by itself is a means of recreating the artistic style, or the stochastic process if you will, of the input texture. While several algorithms have been proposed to synthesize textures, the class of techniques most relevant to our discussion uses nonparametric sampling from example textures to synthesize an arbitrary size texture. This technique was initially popularized by Efros and Leung [2]. Wei and Levoy further enhanced this method with the use of tree-structured vector quantization (TSVQ) to synthesize textures faster [3].

User Guided Texture Synthesis. Ashikhmin modified Wei and Levoy's algorithm to synthesize natural textures by increasing texture coherence. Ashikhmin's algorithm also allowed the user to strategically arrange the texture elements obtained from an input texture by providing a rough color-map of what the output image should look like. Herztmann *et al* combined the algorithms proposed in [1] and [3] to capture artistic style from an image pair consisting of a non-stylized image and the stylized version of the same image [4]. However this technique requires creating or finding a non-stylized version of the image from which the user wants to learn an artistic style, which may not be always possible.

3 Ashikmin's Texture Synthesis Algorithm

Procedure. Ashikhmin's algorithm builds on the texture synthesis algorithm presented by Wei and Levoy [3]. Wei and Levoy propose that each pixel in a texture can be characterized by a small collection of surrounding pixels, or the pixel neighborhood. Their algorithm visits pixels in the output image in raster scan order. For each pixel visited, its value is set equal to the value of the pixel in the input texture that has the most similar neighborhood. The algorithm only considers neighboring pixels that have been already synthesized while constructing a pixel neighborhood. It bootstraps the synthesis by seeding the output image with random pixels drawn from the input texture. The edges of the input and output texture are treated toroidally, meaning pixel neighborhoods that exceed an edge simply wrap across the corresponding-opposite edge.

Instead of searching all the pixels in the input texture to find a target pixel with the most similar neighborhood, Ashikhmin's algorithm constrains the search space to a group of carefully selected candidates. For example, if the pixel one step to the top and left of the current pixel was copied from pixel S in the input image, then the search space includes the pixel in the input texture that has pixel S in the same relative position - one step to the top and left. This creates a list of candidate pixels corresponding to all previously synthesized pixels neighboring the current pixel in the output image. The algorithm then considers only the pixel neighborhoods of the candidate pixels when trying to find the best match for the current pixel. As a result of this constrained search space, the synthesis tends to recreate coherent structures from the input texture.

Ashikhmin's algorithm also allows the user to guide synthesis using a color-map that roughly describes what the output image should look like. Pixel neighborhood comparison is partitioned between the synthesized pixels and pixels in the color-map corresponding to the unsynthesized pixels. The top L-shaped half of the candidate pixel neighborhood is compared to the synthesized pixels in the current pixel neighborhood. The bottom L-shaped half of the candidate pixel neighborhood is compared to the bottom L-shaped neighborhood of the pixel in the color-map corresponding to the current pixel. This encourages texture elements to be placed over regions of similar color in the color-map. The color thus provides the user with some control over the look and feel of the synthesized texture. One can iteratively improve the quality of the synthesized output by using the output from the previous iteration as a color-map for the current iteration. For complete details on the implementation of Ashikhmin's algorithm the reader is referred to the original paper [1].

Improvements. The algorithm can be further enhanced for creating collages by making the following changes:

Neighborhood Construction: While constructing a feature vector from a pixel neighborhood we multiply the pixel neighborhood with a Gaussian kernel centered at the pixel. This gives pixels closer to the current pixel more weight during the candidate search.

User Interaction: Further user interaction can be provided by allowing the user to paint over regions in the synthesized output after each iteration in order to coerce the synthesis to produce the desired output. Another interesting idea is to allow the user to copy a texture patch from the input image to the output while also updating the internal mapping that maps each output pixel to the source pixel in the input image. We would then start the synthesis, in raster scan order, from the middle of this patch and continue throughout the image. Since Ashikhmin's algorithm synthesizes texture by growing patches of textures from the input image, this would provide the user added control over the placement of texture elements in the output.

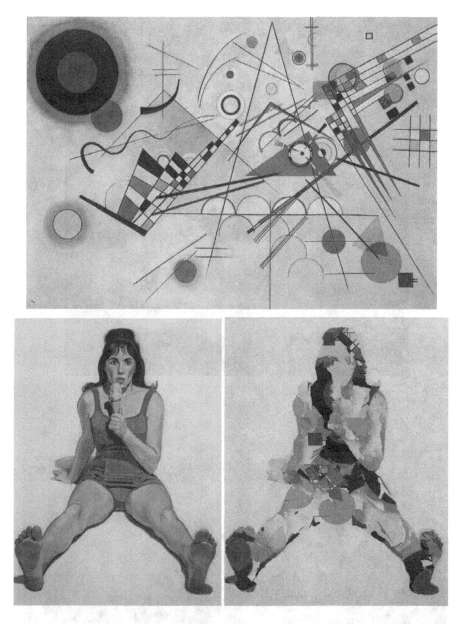

Fig. 1. An automatic collage. We address the problem of recreating an image from elements in the input image using texture synthesis. Here the painting of a lady eating an ice cream cone on the lower left is recreated on the right using the abstract-geometric pieces of the input image on the top.

Fig. 2. Here we recreate a realistic painting by Frederic Bazille using the abstract style of Mordecai Ardon's painting on the top.

4   Results and Conclusion

The results presented in this paper were created using a GIMP plug-in we implemented. We used the stylized source-image as the input texture. We used the image to be reconstructed as the color-map. We used a neighborhood size of 3 x 3 pixels to construct a pixel neighborhood. All results required 15 or fewer iterations to arrive at the final synthesis and the entire process took less than 3 minutes to complete on 2.5 GHz Pentium III processor.

Some artists have already used our plug-in to create finished works or to create reference material. In one case an artist created a set of textures from monoprints (a technique where paint is applied to glass and then pressed to paper) and "applied" the scanned monoprints to photographs. In another case an artist used the algorithm to combine a pair of images. The resulting image was used as a reference for a painting.

References

1. Ashikkmin, M., 2001. "Synthesizing natural textures," *A*CM Symposium on Interactive 3D Graphics, March 2001, pp. 217–226.
2. Efros A. and Leung T., "Texture Synthesis by Non-parametric Sampling," In International Conference on Computer Vision, Vol. 2, September 1999, pp. 1033–1038.
3. Wei L.-Y. and Levoy M., "Fast Texture Synthesis Using Treestructured Vector Quantization," Proceedings of SIGGRAPH 2000, July 2000, pp. 479–488.
4. Hertzmann, A. Jacobs C. E., Oliver N., Curless B., Salesin D. H., "Image Analogies," Proceedings of SIGGRAPH 2001, August 2001, pp. 327—340.

A Method for Smart Graphics in the Web

Thorsten D. Mahler, Stefan A. Fiedler, and Michael Weber

University of Ulm
Department of Media Informatics
Ulm, Germany
{mahler|fiedler|weber}@informatik.uni-ulm.de

Abstract. Shifting the attention from simple static depicting to dynamical generation of visualizations smart graphics can be seen as the next step in the evolution of presentation techniques. A new field of interest for these techniques is the Web which arises the question of how to adopt this new pattern. Based on the Model-View-Controller (MVC) paradigm we developed a generic architecture that allows for user interaction, component separation, adaptivity to environment and user needs and dynamic presentations. By introducing a client side presentational logic component the graphic evolves from a simple presentation to an intelligent visualization that valuates data and presents only the result relevant to the user. We consequently introduce the possibility of completely changing the whole presentation including the user interface by adaptation of the valuation basis. Because this is done by the graphic autonomously the server does not have to be contacted. In order to demonstrate our proposed conceptual approach, we implemented a prototype system by using the techniques available in a Web context.

1 Introduction

Illustrations, images, graphics as they are known today are static presentations used to show concepts, illustrate theories, and present results. In contrast, computers being used as medium to show illustrations provide possibilities that are far beyond this static understanding of graphics.

In this paper we present an approach that utilizes smart graphics for the Web. At first we present a short analysis of the features of smart graphics systems to define the task our conception has to meet. After that we shortly introduce two referenced models and present our approach for a distributed smart graphics system followed by a short description of our prove of concept implementation.

2 Smart Graphics Features

As we focus on an overall conception for smart graphics systems in the Web we firstly present an exemplary selection of smart graphics systems to point out its specialties and advantages included in our approach.

A. Butz et al. (Eds.): SG 2004, LNCS 3031, pp. 146–153, 2004.
© Springer-Verlag Berlin Heidelberg 2004

Visual Map: Visual Map [2] is a project from the area of 3D Geographic Information Systems (GIS). Its goal is to provide the user with an overview on his location by creating a map optimized for his needs. The system is adaptive as it shows the part of the map just needed. It supports orientation by reducing unnecessary information and introducing orientation aids (e.g. landmarks). Furthermore Visual Map is adaptive to hard- and software constraints as well. To achieve this behavior the system has to weigh its input data and to connect it to semantic knowledge about the graphical objects.

WIP/PPP: Primarily WIP/PPP [1] is an authoring system based on a knowledge base which supports the automatic production of multimedia presentations. The modeled life-like characters show, explain, and comment processes and illustrations. The WIP/PPP multimedia authoring system produces an applet which contains all elements and logic for the presentation. WIP/PPP even uses the Web but only to transport the resulting application to the host system - its focus definitely lies on the intelligent interface.

ZoomIllustrator/TextIllustrator: The ZoomIllustrator [7] project and its successor TextIllustrator [4] allow the user to interactively experience 3D-Illustrations. He can explore details of the graphical representation and the system simultaneously provides textual information of the focused object. The textual representation of the portion needed is expanded whenever a more detailed version is required. So this system has to be able to keep both its presentations, graphical and textual, consistent whenever an interaction takes place.

Summarizing these system demonstrate the adaptivity of smart graphics to changes: They are able to recognize requirements and constraints, adapt to users needs and preferences, and react accordingly. They use different approaches to improve the interface; they including domain knowledge in the systems themselves to enable the systems to evaluate semantic knowledge in order to weigh data and react to user interaction. As these are the tasks our method has to meet in the following a smart graphic is defined as a system which is capable of autonomously adapting its presentation to constraints, of valuating changes, and of dynamically updating its visualization accordingly.

3   Reference Models

From a conceptual point of view our work is influenced by two paradigms which are explained in the sequel.

Model-View-Controller: The basic and widely accepted paradigm to model user interaction is the Model-View-Controller (MVC) paradigm [6]. MVC is based on the idea of object orientation and therefore divides an interactive application into three components:

1. A model component which includes the application domain state and behavior, handling all changes of the actual data,
2. A view component responsible for data layout and visualization, and
3. A controller component managing user input and device interaction.

This paradigm enables interactive systems to use different views of the same model at the same time and to keep them synchronously updated. It identifies the functional parts and divides them into independent parts. Therefore, it is a valuable concept for interactive systems. However, the realization of the paradigm is problematic, since especially view and controller have to cooperate closely. In consequence, they can only be separated up to a certain degree [8].

Layout-Content-Logic: The second paradigm our system is based on is the Layout-Content-Logic (LCL) paradigm [5]. This paradigm originates from the area of web engineering and was introduced to solve one of the biggest problems in this field: The commingling of layout, content, and logic.

The mix of content and layout widely has been recognized as disadvantage. The problem of intermingling logic with content or layout is the new aspect that is addressed in this paradigm. Logic in the LCL paradigm refers to the parts responsible for dynamic content creation.

Logic in MVC and LCL: In the MVC paradigm the functional core of the application is the logic contained in the model. In contrast to that the logic component of the LCL paradigm encapsulates the parts responsible for the dynamic content production. So while the LCL logic is purely presentational, the logic contained in the model component of the MVC paradigm is applicational. This differentiation is an important point for smart graphics because they incorporate both: They are interactive systems and use dynamic content creation techniques as they evaluate changes and adapt their presentation likewise.

4   Distributed Smart Graphics

As we are interested in modeling an interactive system our concept will be based on the presented MVC paradigm. However, MVC does not distinguish between applicational and presentational logic. With smart graphics, as stated in Sect. 2, the presentation of the data itself is generated. This functionality neither is part of the MVC model nor is part of the MVC view. We bridge this gap by introducing the presentational logic component that receives the data from the model, processes the presentation data, and passes the newly processed data to the view (see Fig. 1). The separation of applicational and presentational logic allows to procedure the actual presentation as the last step in the chain of data processing and therefore such applications are highly flexible and able to react immediately to interaction.

Fig. 2 depicts the distribution of the identified components, which are explained in the following:

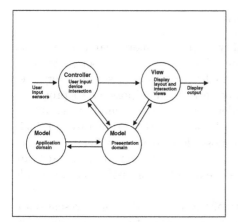

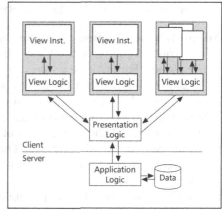

Fig. 1. Enhancement of the MVC architecture for smart graphics.

Fig. 2. Architecture and distribution on client and server.

The Server Side Applicational Logic: The applicational logic is the functional core of the application. It is the only component with direct access to the actual data. As it resides on server side the data can be supervised, protected and shielded from unauthorized access.

Client Side Presentational Logic: The presentational logic acts as the model in the MVC paradigm for the other components. Its task is the communication with the applicational logic to get the data required for presentation and to valuate them afterwards. By adapting the valuation basis the whole presentation can completely be changed. The result of the valuation is passed to the views and an update is initiated. The presentational logic can handle any number of views.

View: The view in this concept is divided into view logic and view instance:

The view logic contains the controller of the MVC paradigm and thus is capable of supporting user interaction. We already know that view and controller have to be tightly coupled. To nevertheless achieve a high degree of independence, we propose to additionally add all logic the view requires to this component. This bears the advantage that the view instance is only a realization of the requested presentation.

The view instance is the realization of the visualization. All visual parts are subsumed in this component. It depends on the view logic, because it holds all the code needed to make this component dynamic. Therefore the view instance and the view logic communicate whenever a change is made, i.e. by changes in the model passed through the presentational logic to the view logic or by changes caused by user interaction with the view.

4.1 Advantages of the Architecture

Adaptation to the user: The possibility of building more than one view and the configurability of the views allows high adaptation to user preferences and needs. For instance a view can be highly configurable, so that every user is able to adapt the view in any way he likes. It is possible to provide a certain number of preset views in order to increase and simplify usability.

Adaptation to the environment: By decoupling the presentational logic from the rest of the system it is also possible to react to different environments and host configurations. The presentational logic can test hardware and software conditions of the host system and accordingly load a suitable view.

Dynamic views: Besides the possibility of static views that just present data, views as well can be dynamic. Here dynamic refers to how view instances are created, i.e. they are produced by a logic part integrated into the view.

Adaptation to presentational tasks: Collaboration of server side and client side logic can be established in order to react to presentational tasks not even known, when the application is loaded. Changes in the underlying model can be made that will have to be visualized. In this case, the presentational logic can request a new visualization from the server and so is able to update the current views.

Application development: A parallel development of view logic and view instances by software developers and e.g. visual artists is possible with this approach. Thus the software developer can focus on programming the logical parts leaving the task of designing the view instances to professional designers that are skilled in the use of special tools for exactly this purpose.

5 Example Implementation

After this conceptional view of smart graphics on the Web we will present an example in order to illustrate the theoretical concepts. On the one hand the reaction to dynamic changes will be demonstrated and we will show the use of different views.

As a demonstrational we chose a spacecraft as technical system and as task the supervision of the life support system. Our implementation constantly receives sensor data from the whole spaceship, which has to be valuated. Finally the visualization has to be presented by the smart graphic.

5.1 Techniques Used in Our Approach

In order to realize our distributed architecture on a wide range of systems, we had to decide how data can be modeled and exchanged between the components and which language is most suitable for programming the logic parts of the smart graphic. Since the implementation should be usable in the Web, it is obvious to decide for standardized web formats and techniques.

For the task of storing and exchanging our different kind of data we use XML, because it has been developed exactly for this purpose. In addition it is a format that is easy to manipulate and open for new standards that are not even yet developed.

As graphic format we chose SVG which is based on XML and therefore profits from many tools available for parsing and processing XML data. Since we opt a web application the choice of the programming language on the client side is restricted by the web browser. Thus we chose ECMAScript over third party solutions like Java applets or plugins. ECMAScript allows the easy integration of all other used formats by standardized procedures via DOM.

5.2   The Presentational Logic

The presentational logic is the central component on the client side. It periodically requests the up-to-date model data from the applicational logic and receives an XML file in response. Thereupon the data is valuated by checking the tolerable ranges denoted in our valuation base. The affected views are informed and an update is triggered using the Subscriber-Notifier [3] concept. It has to be noted that in this stage we are on a purely abstract level. The actual visualization and thus the presentation has to be done by the view.

5.3   The View

The view forms the interface of the application to the user. Its task is the presentation of information to the user and reading interaction from the user.

The View Logic contains all code to react to changes made by the user through interaction and changes initiated by the presentational logic. Every view instance has exactly one view logic, whereas one view logic component can act for more than one view instance.

The View Instance is the part that finally presents a visualization to the user. Conceptually there is more than one way how a view instance is formed. We examined three different kinds of views:

Initial presentation of the view instance: The view contains the displayable view instance. The view logic as a consequence is smaller because it only has to carry out changes on properties of the view instance, while the view instance itself remains unchanged to a large extent. We used this approach to present an initial cutaway of the spaceship to allow a rough diagnosis at a glance. (see Fig. 3, spaceship in background). In our example the view logic reacts to notifications of the presentational logic by changing the background color of the affected room.

View instance by template: The second approach puts more emphasis on the view logic. Nonetheless an initial view instance as static part exists. This initial view instance is not simply shown, but rather used as a template that dynamically is filled with data. This approach has the advantage of being able to use simple and fast tools for template production. We use this method for a second class of views, the inspection windows (see Fig. 3).

Complete generation of the view instance: The final possibility to obtain a presentation is the complete generation of the view instance by the view logic. Initially, the view does not contain a view instance at all. In fact it is generated on demand. This is the most flexible way considering that the view logic has full control of the view instance.

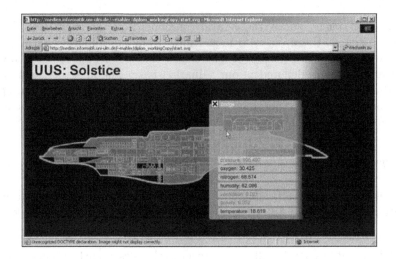

Fig. 3. Our application showing presentations of two different views.

6   Conclusion

Based on the knowledge in the field of web engineering we presented an approach of how to realize and use smart graphics on the Web. Our conception was expected to model a system being able to independently adapt its presentation to conditions, to valuate changes, and to update its visualization accordingly.

Updates are triggered by changing model data and user interaction. Therefore we suggest a conception based on the MVC paradigm and the LCL concept that accomplishes an effective separation of the applicational logic and the view by introducing the presentational logic component. This new component valuates the applicational data before the presentation by the view. Moreover it decides on appropriate visualizations according to environment and user preferences.

Conceptually it provides a separation of the functional parts: The sensitive data remains on the server, where it can be shielded from unauthorized access whereas the presentational components reside on the client. This reduces the web traffic significantly because conventional server based systems have to transfer the whole presentation with every user action. In our approach we transfer in the first step logic together with the presentation to the client, which subsequently can handle changes by itself.

On client side the view only depends on the presentational logic. The views task is the presentation of the valuated data. It is divided into view logic and view instance. The view logic contains the code necessary for operating the view instance. The code includes functions to react to changes in order to dynamically update properties in the view instance and to react to user interaction.

The introduction of smart graphics provides a fortification of the presentation by combining the simple presentation with logic. This leads to a more dynamic and flexible presentation. However, that does not mean that the visualization simply presents dynamic data, it presents a valuated visualization based on the preprocessing of applicational data by the presentational logic. Furthermore a faster development and better reusability can be achieved by the separation of the components.

References

[1] E. André, J. Müller, and T. Rist. WIP/PPP: Knowledge-Based Methods For Automated Multimedia Authoring. In *Proceedings of EUROMEDIA96*, pages 95–102. PUB-SCS, 1996.

[2] V. Coors. Feature-preserving Simplification in Web-based 3D-GIS. In *Proceedings of the International Symposium on Smart Graphics 2001*, pages 22–27. ACM Press, 2001.

[3] E. Gamma, R. Helm, R. Johnson, and J. Vlissides. *Design Patterns: Elements of Reusable Object-Oriented Software*. Addison-Wesley Longman, 11th edition, 1997.

[4] K. Hartmann, S. Schlechtweg, R. Helbing, and T. Strothotte. Knowledge-Supported Graphical Illustration of Texts. In S. L. Maria De Marsico and E. Panizzi, editors, *Proceedings of Working Conference on Advanced Visual Interfaces*, pages 300–307. ACM Press, 2002.

[5] C. Kerer and E. Kirda. Layout, Content and Logic Separation in Web Engineering. In *LNCS 2016 - Web Engineering: Software Engineering and Web Application Development*, pages 135–147. Springer Verlag, 2000.

[6] G. E. Krasner and S. T. Pope. A Cookbook for Using the Model-View-Controller User Interface Paradigm in Smalltalk-80. *Journal of Object Oriented Programming*, 1(3):26–49, Aug./Sept. 1988.

[7] B. Preim, A. Raab, and T. Strothotte. Coherent Zooming of Illustrations with 3D-Graphics and Text. In W. A. Davis, M. Mantei, and R. V. Klassen, editors, *Proceedings of Graphics Interface '97*, pages 105–113. Canadian Information Processing Society, 1997.

[8] Y.-P. Shan. MoDE: A UIMS for Smalltalk. In *Proceedings of the European Conference on Object-Oriented Programming on Object-Oriented Programming Systems, Languages, and Applications (ECOOP/OOPSLA)*, pages 258–268. ACM Press, 1990.

A Framework Supporting General Object Interactions for Dynamic Virtual Worlds

Pieter Jorissen and Wim Lamotte

Expertise Centre for Digital Media
Limburgs Universitair Centrum
Universitaire Campus
B-3590 Diepenbeek, Belgium
{pieter.jorissen, wim.lamotte}@luc.ac.be

Abstract. This work introduces a new interaction framework for dynamic virtual environments. The proposed system is designed to deal with all possible interactions in a virtual world. The idea is to build up a world of objects that contain their own interaction information. As a result the object interactions are application independent and a single scheme is required to handle all interactions in the virtual world. Furthermore, an object model description is designed that provides a means to describe the object's functionality. This description can also be used by AI agents to plan or execute interactions with these objects.

1   Introduction and Related Work

Creating immersive experiences has been a research topic for several years now. Experiencing totally immersive and realistic virtual worlds in which we can interact like in the real world are still not possible. Mixing navigation and meaningful interaction within these virtual environments remains a hard research problem. The actual 3D interactions with objects in a virtual environment (VE) is probably the most important part of computer simulation applications. Current research of interactivity within VEs is however primarily concentrated on user navigation and actor-object interaction using direct interaction techniques ([1][2][3]). As a result, many of the current VEs limit their interactive behavior to executing pre-defined animations when a particular event occurs, or allowing translations and rotations of objects using direct interaction techniques [3]. More advanced actor-object interactions are commonly handled by programming each possibility specifically for each case [4]. This approach is far from general and definitely not runtime adjustable. Using AI techniques to decide what kind of interaction to use and to calculate the necessary parameters to perform it is not yet possible for objects with complex functionality [5]. Furthermore, the way actors (human or AI) should interact with objects in the virtual world is still mostly defined at application level or in predefined scripts describing the actors behavior.

Modelling virtual world objects is a very important part of the VE development process. Though many mechanisms for describing the visual elements of

A. Butz et al. (Eds.): SG 2004, LNCS 3031, pp. 154–158, 2004.
© Springer-Verlag Berlin Heidelberg 2004

objects exist, only a few systems permit the dynamics or interaction properties of the objects to be described as well [6]. A first step into the description of application independent actor-object interaction was taken in [7] where Levinson used an *object specific reasoning module*, creating a relational table to inform actors on object purpose and functionality and used it mainly for simulating the task of grasping. The first time all functional and behavioral information of objects was described at object level was in the *Smart Object* approach presented in [8]. Here, Kallmann et al. propose a framework for general interactions between virtual actors and objects in the virtual world. The idea here is that all information necessary for a virtual actor to interact with an object is included in the object's description. This is achieved by using a combination of pre-defined plans specified through scripted commands. In [9] Smart Objects are used to perform high-level direct interaction with a VR input device. [10] On the other hand uses them in combination with autonomous agents. The Smart Object approach is the only work we found where all object functionality is specified at object level.

Our goal is to create totally dynamic VEs where every object can be interacted with. Also, in contrast with the Smart Object approach, we would like all objects within the virtual world to be able to interact with every other object. We therefore propose a new general interaction scheme for dynamic VEs. We use a similar object functionality description as does the Smart Object approach, but extend it to all objects in the VE. Furthermore, we define a general object interaction scheme that makes no distinction on what kinds of objects (agents, human users or world objects) are interacting, resulting in more dynamic VEs allowing also for object-object and object-actor interactions.

2   Architecture

In this section we discuss the approach we followed in the design of our general VE interaction framework. First we describe how our objects and their interaction features are modelled. Then, we present how interaction between these objects occurs, and how the virtual world is constructed.

2.1   Interactive Objects

Our starting point was the view given in [11]:

> How different interaction requests are processed, as well as how many participants may interact with an object concurrently, is highly dependent on the object itself.

We therefore created objects composed of parts, where each part can have its own animations, actions and constraints. Inter-part constraints, state dependant constraints, actions and animations on the other hand are specified at object level. Object variables can be defined to store data or state information. The interaction properties of the objects define how interactions can be triggered and what functionality is invoked. The objects triggers and acceptable commands are defined here. Triggering occurs for example when something collides with a defined interaction zone (collision trigger) of an object, when a command is received from another object (command trigger) or when a certain time is reached (time trigger). How an object reacts to a trigger or a called command is described in the behavior part of its description. Triggers can be used to invoke actions as well as behaviors. Actions are defined as combinations of object part movements or movements of the object itself, over a certain time. Behaviors on the other hand are described in a scripting language and can be used to initiate more advanced interaction behavior such as collision handling or the triggering of other objects behavior. Scripts can access object variables and can initiate actions, animations and other behaviors. It would even be possible to describe AI agent behavior.

The main advantage of this approach is that all the information needed to interact with an object is located at the object level and not at the application level. As a result, the objects or their parts are easy to modify, even at runtime. Secondly, the objects are easy to reuse in other applications or just partly for the construction of other interactive objects. Finally, a connection with high-level planners is naturally achieved.

2.2   Interactive Worlds

To create totally dynamic virtual worlds, we build up our world only from the interactive objects described in the previous section. Objects are interconnected by links that create a structure for the world and provide a means of communication. An interaction layer is responsible for creating and maintaining the objects in the virtual environment. It is the central control unit for all object interaction in the VE. First of all it creates necessary links between objects and maintains these for as long as they are required. The most important links the interaction layer can create are contact links, attach links, controller links and parent/child links. Secondly the interaction layer is responsible for checking all object triggers. Furthermore it is responsible for the actual execution of object functionality (scripts and actions). As an example, consider the case where an object hits another object while moving. When the collision occurs, a *contact link* between the objects is set up by the interaction layer. The object then sends a *move* message containing the movement parameters through the link. The interaction layer then checks the contact and movement behavior and constraints of all objects that are connected through contact and attach links. It then calculates what behavior is possible for all the objects involved, calculates the parameters and triggers all necessary behavior. If in the next step (after movement and the first step of the triggered behavior of all the object) the objects are no longer in touch, the contact link is removed.

All interactions in the VE happen according to this scheme. To manipulate an object in a VE, a controller can be attached to it. A controller is a higher-level part of the application, which takes for example user input or output from an AI module and converts it into commands that are sent to the object. A controller is connected to an object by a controller link, which makes it possible to send commands to the objects via the interaction layer. This approach is very different from the Smart Objects where actors (human or AI) are not subjected to the same interaction rules as the objects they manipulate. As a result our interaction scheme is a lot more general and the only one necessary for an entire interactive VE. Of course more work is necessary in the modelling stage, but reusability and flexibility of designed objects by far outweighs this disadvantage.

3 Conclusions and Future Work

We presented a new interaction framework capable of handling all interactions in a VE. The general interaction scheme uses objects containing their own interaction information and behavior. Links between objects are used to structure the world and to allow for communication. A special interaction layer controls all objects and is responsible for the links between them and the handling of the triggering of all their behavior. By treating all parts of VEs (actors, objects and the world itself) equally, our interaction scheme is far more general than the Smart Object approach.

Currently we have a basic implementation of the interactive object framework, containing a basic script engine that can access object information and variables, call animations and other interaction behaviors. The framework was tested with a few objects with fairly simple behavior with very positive results. We will perform more specified tests with more advanced objects soon. After this, we would like to extend our script engine to support more advanced instructions, allowing interactive AI agents to be introduced in our VEs. Afterwards, we would like to extend our general framework to work for distributed VEs as well. This will be achieved by adding information for simultaneous access to the object description and extending the interactive layer to resolve problems that occur when the virtual world is distributed over a network. The main goal here would be to create dynamic networked VEs where object access is defined at object level instead of by a global floor control mechanism.

4 Acknowledgments

Part of this research was funded by the IWT project number 020339 and the Flemish Government.

References

[1] Hand, C.: A Survey of 3D Interaction Techniques. Computer Graphics Forum 16(5) (1997) 269–281
[2] Mine, M., Jr., F.B., Sequin, C.: Moving Objects in Space Exploiting Proprioception in Virtual Environment Interaction. In: Proceedings of SIGGRAPH'97, Los Angeles (1997)

[3] Bowman, D.: Interaction Techniques for Common Tasks in Immersive Virtual Environments: Design, Evaluation and Application. PhD thesis, Georgia Institute of Technology (1999)

[4] Smith, S., Duke, D., Willans, J.: Designing World Objects for Usable Virtual Environments. In: Workshop on Design, Specification and Verification of Interactive Systems (DSVIS'00). (2000) 309–319

[5] Parisy, O., Schlick, C.: A physically Realistic Framework for the Generation of High-Level Animation Controllers. In: Proceedings of the 2nd international symposium on Smart Graphics, (Hawthorne, New York) 47–54

[6] Pettifer, S.: An Operating Environment for Large Scale Virtual Reality. PhD thesis, University of Manchester (1999)

[7] Levinson, L.: Connecting Planning and Acting: Towards an Architecture for Object-Specific Reasoning. PhD thesis, University of Pennsylvania (1996)

[8] Kallmann, M., Thalmann, D.: Modeling Objects for Interactive Tasks. In: EGCAS'98 - 9th Eurographics Workshop on Animation and Simulation, Lisbon (1998)

[9] Kallmann, M., Thalmann, D.: Direct 3D Interaction with Smart Objects. In: Proceedings of ACM VRST'99, London (1999)

[10] Gonçalvez, L., Kallmann, M., Thalmann, D.: Programming Behaviors with Local Perception and Smart Objects: an Approach to Solve Autonomous Agents Tasks. In: XIV Brazilian Symposium on Computer Graphics and Image Processing, Florianópolis (2001)

[11] Broll, W.: Interacting in Distributed Collaborative Virtual Environments. In: Proceedings of the IEEE Virtual Reality International Symposium, Los Almitos (1995) 148–155

The Media Lounge: a Software Platform for Streamed 3D Interactive Mixed Media

Marc Price

BBC Research and Development
Kingswood Warren, Tadworth, Surrey KT20 6NP, UK
marc.price@rd.bbc.co.uk

Abstract. The future 'Media Lounge' is a demonstration application which is being developed to provide a better understanding of what can be achieved with streamed 3D interactive mixed media in the home. It demonstrates how conventional broadcast media (digital radio and digital television) can be embedded into shared 3D interactive environments, with the aid of the home network. The idea is to enhance the radio listening and TV viewing experience, by combining it with a shared virtual world.

1   Introduction

The broadband-enabled, networked 'home platform' will offer an unprecedented range of features. The idea of being able to interconnect a TV set-top box, a PC, a games console, and on a wider scale, home networks of other households, brings to life a new shared experience of streamed 3D interactive mixed media.

From the outset, it is difficult to define exactly what the best way of exploiting these features might be. Nevertheless, the broadcaster would be negligent to ignore this imminent convergence of media technologies. From the BBC's perspective, the development of the home platform needs to be driven according to the needs of the user. A small group of engineers at BBC Research and Development have been actively pursuing this for the past 12 months, by exploring the use of computer game technology as the basis of the future home platform. The planned outcome of this work is a number of demonstration applications which will show a variety of ways this mixture of technologies can be exploited.

The demonstration system described in this paper is called the 'Media Lounge'. It demonstrates the use of a networked, computer game engine (we are currently using the 'Crystal Space' open source game SDK [1]) to mix streamed audio and video content with 3D interactive content. The idea is to exploit 3D game hardware and software to enhance the TV viewing, or radio listening, experience. It builds upon the phenomenon of ad-hoc communities that have evolved around networked/online computer games. In section 2, the motivation for this particular application is discussed, followed in section 3, by a description of the system functionality. Finally, section 4 discusses specific usage scenarios.

A. Butz et al. (Eds.): SG 2004, LNCS 3031, pp. 159–163, 2004.
© Springer-Verlag Berlin Heidelberg 2004

2 Motivation

Our primary motivation for creating this application is simply to demonstrate how the home network provides for new and multiple modes of mixed media. In order to achieve this objective, the demonstration must also have the potential to be of substantial social benefit. In the case of the 'Media Lounge', this benefit can be concisely described as: "To add value to existing broadcast services". However, this statement hides the real benefits of the 'Media Lounge'.

It is important to note that radio and TV programmes, be they informational or pure entertainment, often provide a talking point for groups of people - friends, family, colleagues, etc. This is quite a subtle point, but it helps fulfill the human desire to communicate and interact with others. There needs to be a reason to hold a conversation, in order for that conversation to lead to a colourful social interaction and expression. The weather just does not suffice!

Family shows and sports commentaries involve the listener/viewer as an audience member, uniting friends and family members to a common subject, hence facilitating a necessary sense of togetherness. Documentaries provoke intellectual discussion. Drama provides for a group experience of immersion. However, there are many social situations when these benefits of straight forward radio and TV cannot be attained. The doting parent, away from their family on business; the child that lives a long way from her school friends - or indeed, the child that has been 'grounded'; the student who studies at a college a long way from home; the professional who has moved far afield for their career; the sick child, who is isolated in hospital. These examples illustrate how people in such situations miss their friends or their family, and they miss being able to share the experience of radio and TV.

Of course, it is not just radio and TV that provide a powerful shared experience. There is also the experience of game. The networked or online computer game has allowed such shared experiences to transcend the boundaries of the locality and become worldwide events. As such, ad-hoc virtual communities surrounding popular games have arisen, where conversational subject matter has quickly moved onto more pressing subjects than the latest cheat codes, or how many monsters you have killed. 'In' jokes, and other subtle references to features of gameplay and content often appear in the conversations, but the essential subject matter is important topical conversation.

This phenomenon began with computer games like 'Quake' [2], which allowed small groups of players to play the game together over the internet, via an internet-based server. The communities that arose from this exchanged emails in addition to the small-talk that they made via the game itself. In the present day, online games exist whose business mainly rests on the communities that they create (eg [3]). The 'Media Lounge' seeks to build on the game-related virtual community phenomenon, by allowing internet users to also share their radio and TV programme experiences remotely.

3 System Functionality

Upon invocation, the Media Lounge downloads a 3D virtual world from an appropriate server. The virtual world consists of buildings - perhaps a city - and natural features. Each room of the buildings is a 'virtual mixed-media lounge'. The application also connects with a local DVB-server process, that is hosted on the home-networked, digital set-top box - at its simplest, this would be a DVB card installed in a PC attached to the home network. The DVB server streams all broadcast audio and video content requested by the Media Lounge application, over the local home network. Each virtual mixed-media lounge within the downloaded 3D world contains a virtual TV/radio. This is actually represented in the content as an appropriately shaped polygon with a tag to identify its A/V source - essentially, the tag is a channel ident. The Media Lounge application detects each tag, and maps the appropriate streamed video and audio content into the virtual environment, at the relevant locations. The user selects the desired lounge, and hence the desired channel, by navigating through the virtual world.

The Media Lounge application functions similarly to a networked game engine. It can be instructed by the user to act as a 'server', to allow a small group of elected 'friends' to connect and share the same virtual world. Alternatively, it can be instructed to be a 'client', where it searches on the internet for all other active Media Lounge applications that are in 'server' mode, and reports those that it has permission to connect with - ie it checks whether the user has been elected as a 'friend'. Hence, the broadband connection allows the user to interact with other occupants of the virtual world, creating a shared mixed-media experience beyond the boundaries of the user's real room. The interactions could use any type of available interface, such as motion, text, speech, video, etc. However, the demonstration system in its current state simply uses text.

Each occupant of a room is assigned an avatar. At any point in time, the avatar is located according to the position of the viewpoint that the corresponding occupant has adopted. The avatar itself would be some form of 3D humanoid model. In its most simplest form, this model could consist of a blank rectangle, showing the users name or a recent photograph, and the most recent text input from them. However, we would use a video texture-mapped polygon actor model technique, as used in PROMETHEUS [4]. This creates a human model by inserting simple geometry (a rectangle, or a semi-spheroidal polygon) into the virtual environment and texture-mapping it with a live video. The video input comes from a webcam pointing at the corresponding user, which is encoded into a video stream.

The images in Fig. 1 are snap-shots of the Media Lounge application. Here, we see different viewpoints of a Virtual Media Lounge in a wooden floored, stone building. The virtual TV is tuned to BBC2.

Fig. 1. Views of a virtual mixed-media lounge

4   System Usage

It is interesting to consider the usage and content development for the 'Media Lounge' with specific scenarios in mind.

As it stands, the system is likely to be popular with fans of cult TV and radio programmes, for which virtual worlds could be specifically created. For example, 'Doctor Who' fans would probably enjoy watching episodes from within a virtual 'TARDIS', in the company of like-minded individuals [5]. The virtual world could also be themed according to the events of the current episode. For example, the audience of the first episode of 'The Hitchhikers Guide to the Galaxy' might find themselves listening to it in Arthur Dent's local pub, while the last episode's audience might listen from the 'Restaurant at the End of the Universe' [6].

This technique of matching 3D content to programme could be exploited for other genres. For example, interior design 'make-over' TV programmes could be watched from inside the featured building. Live audience shows could be experienced from inside the studio. It would also work particularly well with music shows. The virtual world could be designed with a club-like atmosphere, in the style most fitting the music genre. Participants could interact as they might in a real club: contemplating, chatting, or even dancing together, with the aid of 'Dance Mats'.

5   Summary

This review has described an application which demonstrates one way in which conventional broadcast media can be embedded into shared 3D interactive environments. The motivation for the application, its functionality, and its usage were discussed.

References

1. http://crystal.sf.net
2. http://www.idsoftware.com

3. http://thesimsonline.ea.com
4. M.Price, et al, 'Real-time Production and Delivery of 3D Media', *Proceedings of International Broadcasting Convention*, 2002.
5. http://www.bbc.co.uk/cult/doctorwho/
6. http://www.bbc.co.uk/cult/hitchhikers/

Author Index